READING AND VOCABULARY 1

Focus

Jo McEntire

Series Consultant
Lawrence J. Zwier

NATIONAL GEOGRAPHIC LEARNING | CENGAGE Learning®

Australia • Brazil • Japan • Korea • Mexico • Singapore • Spain • United Kingdom • United States

NATIONAL GEOGRAPHIC LEARNING | **CENGAGE Learning**

Reading and Vocabulary Focus 1

Jo McEntire

Publisher: Sherrise Roehr

Series Consultant: Lawrence J. Zwier

Executive Editor: Laura Le Dréan

Contributing Editors: Bernard Seal and Jennifer Bixby

Director of Global Marketing: Ian Martin

Product Marketing Manager: Lindsey Miller

Director, Content and Media Production: Michael Burggren

Senior Content Project Manager: Daisy Sosa

Print Buyer: Mary Beth Hennebury

Cover Designers: Christopher Roy and Michael Rosenquest

Cover Image: Hiroyuki Matsumoto/ Photographer's Choice/Getty Images

Text Design and Layout: Don Williams

Composition: Page Designs International

Copyright © 2014 National Geographic Learning, a part of Cengage Learning

ALL RIGHTS RESERVED. No part of this work covered by the copyright herein may be reproduced, transmitted, stored, or used in any form or by any means graphic, electronic, or mechanical, including but not limited to photocopying, recording, scanning, digitizing, taping, Web distribution, information networks, or information storage and retrieval systems, except as permitted under Section 107 or 108 of the 1976 United States Copyright Act, or applicable copyright law of another jurisdiction, without the prior written permission of the publisher.

For product information and technology assistance, contact us at
**Cengage Learning Customer & Sales Support,
1-800-354-9706**
For permission to use material from this text or product,
submit all requests online at **www.cengage.com/permissions**.
Further permissions questions can be e-mailed to
permissionrequest@cengage.com.

Student Book ISBN: 978-1-285-17319-1

National Geographic Learning
20 Channel Center Street
Boston, MA 02210
USA

Cengage Learning is a leading provider of customized learning solutions with office locations around the globe, including Singapore, the United Kingdom, Australia, Mexico, Brazil and Japan.

Cengage Learning products are represented in Canada by Nelson Education, Ltd.

Visit National Geographic Learning online at **NGL.cengage.com**

Visit our corporate website at **www.cengage.com**

Printed in the United States of America
3 4 5 6 7 8   19 18 17 16 15 14

CONTENTS

TRAVEL

FIRE AND WATER

THE POWER OF IDEAS

CONTENTS (CONTINUED)

Each unit opens with an amazing **National Geographic** image that taps into learners' natural curiosity about the world while introducing the content that will be explored in the readings.

A comprehensive, three-part **vocabulary development program** builds student confidence as learners meet new or unfamiliar words in academic texts.

READING 2   CLEAN TRAVEL

Each one of us shares this planet with seven billion other individuals. And we all need transportation. People and products need to move from city to city and country to country. However, the majority of cars, motorcycles, boats, and planes cause pollution. They are also noisy. This is a serious problem in many cities. So inventors are coming up with innovative ideas to try to reduce the pollution and noise. Their ideas are not yet perfect. However, all great ideas begin somewhere.

SOLARIMPULSE

By Land

In many cities around the world, motorcycles are becoming increasingly popular. Currently, Vietnam has around 33 million motorcycles. China has almost 120 million. Motorcycles are a faster and cheaper way to get around a city than cars. Yet the convenience of these motorcycles comes at a cost. Air pollution is a growing problem. In large cities, people often complain it is difficult to breathe. They also complain about the noise.

To solve these problems, a U.S. company designed an environmentally friendly motorcycle. It uses electricity as fuel. As a result, there is no pollution. You can drive it for 40 miles (64 kilometers) before recharging the battery. It is also quiet and fast—60 miles (96 kilometers) per hour. This makes it a good choice for getting around a city.

By Water

The Italian city of Venice is a city with only a few roads. There are no cars in the city center. Instead of cars, water taxis and buses carry people along the city's canals. The engines of these boats are simple and cheap. However, they cause pollution, particularly to the water. This causes damage to the city's buildings.

English mechanics Dick Strawbridge and Jem Stans designed a solar-powered water taxi. The solar panels charge three electric batteries. These, in turn, provide power to the engine. The water taxi can carry six passengers. It can run for a day. In the future, solar taxis could be an alternative to Venice's current taxis.

By Air

Designing an environmentally friendly airplane is a real challenge. Planes use an enormous amount of jet fuel. This means they cause significant air pollution, and they are very noisy. Some major airplane manufacturers have started to address the problems. They are using cleaner fuels, for example. However, Swiss engineers have gone one step further. They developed a solar airplane—the *Solar Impulse*. Solar panels cover its wings. These panels provide power to four electric motors and batteries. The batteries allow the plane to fly at night. This plane holds the world record for the longest solar-powered flight—958 miles (1,541 kilometers) from Arizona to Texas in the United States.

READING COMPREHENSION

Big Picture

A Choose the answer that best completes each of the following sentences.

1. The main idea of paragraph 2 is that _____ .
   a. China and Vietnam have around 155 million motorcycles
   b. motorcycles are noisy and cause air pollution

2. The main idea of paragraph 3 is that _____ .
   a. a new motorcycle is pollution-free
   b. a new electric motorcycle can reach 60 miles per hour

3. The main idea of paragraph 4 is that _____ .
   a. Venice is an unusual city
   b. boats are causing pollution in Venice

4. The main idea of paragraph 5 is that _____ .
   a. the solar-powered water taxi may be a good alternative to water taxis in use today
   b. the soar-powered water taxi can carry up to six people

5. The main idea of paragraph 6 is that _____ .
   a. planes use an enormous amount of jet fuel
   b. the *Solar Impulse* is good for the environment because it uses solar power instead of jet fuel

Content-rich readings supported by real-world images, maps, charts, and informational graphics prepare learners for academic success.

After each reading . . .

READING COMPREHENSION

Big Picture

A The following statements are the main ideas of each paragraph in Reading 1. Write the correct paragraph number next to its main idea.

_____ 1. Wadongo realized that students without electricity did not do well in school.

_____ 2. Wadongo's parents encouraged him to work hard in school.

_____ 3. Wadongo began to build more solar lamps.

_____ 4. Kerosene lamps cause serious problems.

_____ 5. Solar lamps improve the lives of rural families.

_____ 6. Wadongo developed a lamp that is good for the environment.

_____ 7. Wadongo was able to keep the cost of the lamps down.

B Compare answers to Exercise A with a partner. Then discuss what you think the main idea of the whole reading is.

Close-Up

Choose the answer that best completes each of the following sentences.

1. Wadongo was unhappy at school because _____ .
   a. he had to drop out before he could finish
   b. he knew he could get better grades
   c. he was not as intelligent as the other students
   d. he did not have a solar lamp

2. According to the reading, children sometimes leave school because they _____ .
   a. do not like learning
   b. cannot pay for their school
   c. find it difficult to study without electricity
   d. do not have enough kerosene lamps

3. Solar lamps are good for the environment because _____ .
   a. they are free
   b. they do not use kerosene
   c. people can see better with these lamps
   d. they only cost $20 to make

4. Wadongo was able to keep the cost down because _____ .
   a. he was a student at a university
   b. he knew the lamps had to be inexpensive
   c. the people who built the lamps worked for free
   d. he paid an organization to help build the lamps

5. According to the reading, Wadongo thinks that _____ .
   a. solar lamps are a long-term solution
   b. rural families will never have electricity
   c. these lamps are only a short-term solution
   d. solar lamps are a better solution than electricity because they are free

Reading Comprehension sections assess learner comprehension through a variety of activities.

Learners are taught an essential **reading skill** and then apply that skill meaningfully to the reading.

Reading Skill

Identifying Supporting Details

In Unit 2, you learned that writers use specific details to support the main idea of a paragraph. (See page 30.) Supporting details are usually facts (names, numbers), reasons, and examples. Writers often use signals to introduce supporting details:

first, next, also, in addition, finally, lastly
for example, for instance, such as, including
one reason, experts believe, research shows

To identify supporting details:
- look for the main idea and highlight it
- look for signals that introduce supporting details that explain this main idea
- check that the details are specific, not general information

Note: Not all sentences in a paragraph provide supporting details. Writers often give background information to help you understand the topic. This information is often in the beginning of the paragraph.

A Read the following paragraph. As you read, underline the main idea. Number the supporting details. Then answer the questions below.

¹In India, over 400 million people have no access to electricity. ²This is a serious problem for several reasons. ³First, without electricity, children cannot study easily. ⁴Without education, they cannot get good jobs. ⁵Next, without electricity, people can't use computers and do not have access to the Internet. ⁶As a result, they don't learn important technology skills. ⁷Finally, without electricity, people stay home in the evenings. ⁸They do not go out to places such as shops, restaurants, and movie theaters. ⁹This means businesses do not develop and grow.

1. Which sentence provides the main idea? _____
2. Which sentence provides background information to the main idea? _____
3. Which signal words does the writer use? _____
4. Write the supporting details: _____

Academic Vocabulary sections develop the language that students are likely to encounter in authentic academic readings.

VOCABULARY PRACTICE

Academic Vocabulary

A Find the words in the box in Reading 1. Use the context and the words in parentheses to help you choose the correct word to complete each of the following sentences.

| encouraged (Par. 1) | materials (Par. 6) | estimates (Par. 7) |
| rural (Par. 1) | volunteers (Par. 6) | impact (Par. 7) |

1. The United Nations _____ (guesses) that about 25 percent of the world does not have access to electricity.

2. In Bihar, India, the majority of people who live in _____ (farming) areas have no electrical power in their homes.

3. Having no electricity can have a very serious _____ (effect) on families in Bihar.

4. To try to solve this problem, the Indian government _____ (supported) research companies to work in Bihar.

5. _____ (unpaid workers) from these companies try to find inexpensive ways to bring electricity to farming areas.

6. One company, Husk Power Systems, has found a way to turn waste _____ (something you need to make other things) from rice into electricity.

B Work with a partner and complete each sentence with a word from the box. The correct word often appears with the word in bold. Give reasons for your choices.

| areas | experts | help | huge | parents | recycled |

1. In many schools, **volunteers** _____ young children learn to read.

2. Energy _____ **estimate** that the cost of gas will rise to more than six dollars a gallon by the end of the year.

3. People who live in **rural** _____ often grow some or all of their own food.

4. _____ **encourage** their children to study hard at school.

5. Education can have a(n) _____ **impact** on a child's life.

6. Many companies now use _____ **materials** to make new products.

Multiword Vocabulary sections identify words that are commonly grouped together and then prompt learners to work with them in different contexts for enhanced comprehension.

B The box below contains academic words from Exercise A and words they often appear with. Complete each sentence with a phrase from the box.

| air transportation | a good alternative | provide jobs |
| design a product | innovative ways | significant changes |

1. When companies _____, they have to think about who will use it, how easily it works, and how much it will cost.

2. People who are worried about the environment believe that we need more _____ to solve the problems connected with oil-based energy.

3. Technology has led to _____ in education. For example, students now learn very advanced computer skills at an early age.

4. The cost of _____ is very closely connected to the cost of oil. When oil prices increase, the cost of tickets usually increases as well.

5. Residents hope that the new factory will _____ in the area. This would help the many people who are looking for work.

6. More electric cars are now available. These cars are _____ to traditional, gas-based cars.

Multiword Vocabulary

Find the multiword vocabulary in bold in Reading 2. Then use the context and the sentences below to choose the correct answers.

1. Cell phones **are becoming increasingly popular** (Par. 2) because they can connect to the Internet and can take photos and videos.
   a. are being used a lot
   b. are being used more and more

2. I love my city because it is easy **to get around** (Par. 2) by foot and by bus.
   a. travel
   b. learn to drive

3. More people today have a car than in the past. However, this **comes at a cost** (Par. 2) to the environment.
   a. helps
   b. causes problems

4. Because bicycles are **environmentally friendly,** (Par. 3) cities are encouraging more people to use this form of transportation.
   a. fun to ride
   b. good for the earth

5. Cities are beginning to **address the problems** (Par. 6) of pollution by using more solar-powered buses and trains.
   a. solve the challenges
   b. understand the problems

6. Who has the **world record** (Par. 6) for winning the most Olympic gold medals?
   a. the biggest number
   b. the average number

Use the Vocabulary

Write answers to the following questions. Use the words in bold in your answers. Then share your answers with a partner.

1. What kinds of cars are **becoming increasingly popular** right now? Why do you think people like this type of car?

2. How can an individual live in an **environmentally friendly** way? Make a list of the things you can do to live in this way.

3. How do you **get around** your community? Do you use **public transportation**? Why or why not?

4. Think about a country or a city you have visited. What are some of the **significant** differences between that country or city and the place where you grew up?

5. Pollution from cars and motorbikes is a problem in almost every country. What are some governments doing to **address this problem**?

6. The Internet **provides** a huge amount of information. What kind of information do you search for on a daily basis?

7. Solar power is called an "**alternative**" fuel because it's not coal and it's not made from petroleum. What other types of alternative fuels are there?

In **Use the Vocabulary**, students get to activate the newly-learned vocabulary in new and interesting contexts.

THINK AND DISCUSS

Work in a small group. Use the information in the reading and your own ideas to discuss the following questions.

1. **Analyze.** What challenges face engineers as they try to design better forms of transportation?
2. **Identify problems.** What are some of the disadvantages, or problems, of an electric motorcycle, solar water taxi, and the *Solar Impulse*?
3. **Express an opinion.** How will methods of transportation change in the future?

Clean Travel **61**

Think and Discuss questions at the end of each reading require learners to discuss their opinions on the topic while making connections to their own lives.

The **Vocabulary Review** recycles the key vocabulary from the unit and offers meaningful, contextualized practice opportunities.

UNIT REVIEW

Vocabulary Review

A Complete the paragraphs with the vocabulary below that you have studied in the unit.

| comes at a cost | experts estimate | keeps the cost down | instead of |
| dropped out of school | huge impact | innovative way | recycled materials |

United Nations _____ that in Africa and Asia the average woman has to
walk six kilometers every day for clean water. In Ethiopia, Aylito Binayo is one of these women. Each
day, she leaves her rural home and walks for hours to get to clean water. It is hard, tiring work, and
it _____. Carrying heavy water causes a lot of injuries and takes a lot of time.

In South Africa, Piet Hendrikse watched many women and children fetching water. He saw the
_____ this had on their health. He knew that many girls even
_____ to fetch water for their parents. So he came up with
a simple idea. He designed the Q-Drum. This is a large, plastic drum with
a hole in the middle. A woman fills it with 50 liters of water. Then she
puts a rope through the hole. _____ carrying the
water, she pulls it.

Q-Drums are becoming increasingly popular, and not just in
Africa. Hendrikse's company is helping people in other countries to
make these drums. He encourages them to use
_____. This _____ because
the company doesn't have to buy many new materials. The Q-Drum is
definitely a simple, but _____ to carry water.

The Q-drum

B Compare answers to Exercise A with a partner. Then discuss the following questions.
What are some of the effects of having no access to safe, clean water? Do you agree that the Q-Drum is an innovative idea?

C Complete the following sentences in a way that shows that you understand the meaning of the words in bold.

1. Parents should **encourage** their children to _____
2. After a fire destroyed several apartments, **volunteers helped** the families find _____
3. _____ all help us **get around** cities easily.
4. For two years, I tried to get a job in Paris, but then I **gave up** and _____

D Work with a partner and write four sentences that include any four of the vocabulary items below. You may use any verb tense and make nouns plural if you want.

air transportation	get rid of	provide jobs
become increasingly popular	a good alternative	world record
environmentally friendly		

Connect the Readings

A The readings in this unit describe some serious global problems. They discuss some of the results of these problems, and they talk about some solutions.

1. Use information from Readings 1 and 2 to complete the following chart.

Problem	Results	Solution
They don't have electricity at home.		They drop out of school.
Kerosene lamps burn easily.		Solar lamp
Kerosene is expensive.		
	It causes problems with eyes and illnesses.	Solar lamp
Rural Kenyan families do not have a lot of money.	They can't afford expensive solar lamps.	
		Inventors are coming up with ideas to reduce pollution.
Venice relies on boats.		
Planes use a lot of jet fuel.		
Motorcycles		

2. Work with a partner. Think about the following ideas. What problems might happen as a result of these ideas? The first one has been done for you.

Idea	Problem
Solar lamps	*Families do not have electricity for a phone or for cooking*
Volunteers build the solar lamps	
Solar-powered water taxis	
Electric motorcycles	
Solar-powered planes	

B With a partner or in a small group, compare answers to Exercise A. Then discuss the following questions.

1. Readings 1 and 2 explore some serious problems. Which do you think is the most serious problem?
2. Which is the most creative solution?

C Discuss the following questions with a partner. Use your understanding of the readings and your own ideas.

1. Some car companies offer electric cars as a good alternative to gas cars. However, not very many people buy electric cars. Why?
2. Think of another global problem. Are people finding innovative solutions to this problem?

Connect the Readings sections at the end of each unit practice critical thinking skills as learners are guided to compare, contrast, and synthesize information from the two readings.

SERIES INTRODUCTION

Welcome to National Geographic Learning's new Reading and Vocabulary Focus *series. The series delivers memorable reading experiences, develops essential reading skills, and showcases a wide variety of high-utility vocabulary. The passages take readers to exciting new places where they can apply the skills of successful academic readers. While engaged with the content, readers encounter target vocabulary that is ample, diverse, and presented with a fresh, pragmatic view of what the term vocabulary item truly means.*

Great reading classes depend on top-of-the-line content. That's why we've taken such great care in selecting content for *Reading and Vocabulary Focus*. Through all four levels (high beginning to low advanced), *Reading and Vocabulary Focus* draws from the vast resources of National Geographic. High-interest reading content written by some of the world's most authoritative and thought-provoking reporters and explorers is presented in level-appropriate language and used to build reading skills and to promote vocabulary learning. Skill building is of course important, but not for its own sake. Our goal is always, first and foremost, for students to enjoy working with readings that are truly interesting and worth reading.

A BROADBAND APPROACH TO VOCABULARY

A distinctive feature of *Focus* is its broadband approach to vocabulary. For each reading passage, three groups of vocabulary are called out:

1) 10–12 topic-related vocabulary items to consider in pre-reading activities
2) 6–8 academic words—single word items essential to building an academic vocabulary
3) 6–8 multiword vocabulary items useful in academic reading

A systematic focus on multiword vocabulary sets *Reading and Vocabulary Focus* apart from most reading/vocabulary texts. Increasingly, more and more teachers and many textbooks recognize that some vocabulary items consist of more than one word, especially phrasal/prepositional verbs (*hurry up, take on*) and compound nouns (*glass ceiling, weather station*). However, the amount of effort and text space devoted to expanding students' multiword repertoires is typically minimal and the approach haphazard.

Our thinking in the *Reading and Vocabulary Focus* series has been influenced by numerous researchers who have examined the great importance to native speakers of conventionalized multi-word units, whether those units are called "chunks," "strings," or something else. Schmitt and Carter settle on the term *formulaic sequences* and point out a helpful description by Wray, that formulaic sequences "are stored and retrieved whole from memory at the time of use rather than being subject to generation and analysis at the time of use by the language grammar." (Schmitt & Carter, 2012, 13)[1]

It is not always easy to decide whether a group of words constitutes a unit so tight and useful that it should be taught as a discrete vocabulary item. In our item selection for *Focus*, we applied the criterion of "stored and retrieved whole." An item could make the cut if, in the expert judgment of our authors and editors, it was probably treated cognitively as a whole thing. In this way, we were able to judge that such diverse language as *pay attention to*, *on the whole*, *an invasion of privacy*, and *be the first to admit* are formulaic sequences that learners should study and learn as whole units. We checked our judgment against as many sources as possible, including corpora such as the Bank of English (part of the Collins COBUILD corpus) and the online version of the *Corpus of Contemporary American English* (COCA).[2]

UNIT STRUCTURE

Each unit of *Reading and Vocabulary Focus* begins with a high-impact photograph related to the unit theme to capture the students' imaginations and allow for pre-reading discussion. The unit theme encourages inquiry and exploration and offers opportunities for synthesis of information. Two reading passages, related to each other thematically, form the heart of the unit. Each reading is followed by stages of comprehension work, reading skill practice, formative vocabulary exercises, and discussion. Finally the unit ends with a comprehensive vocabulary review section and critical thinking synthesizing tasks.

Pre-Reading and Reading

For each reading passage, pre-reading activities include a task that activates content schemata and a vocabulary exercise that provides a set of clues to the content that the reader will encounter while reading. Each reading has been chosen for high-interest and conceptual challenge and is presented in the company of some of the world's most stimulating photography and other graphics.

Comprehension and Vocabulary Development

Comprehension exercises after each reading start out with a focus on main ideas ("Big Picture") and move to details ("Close-Up"). Then a concise treatment of a high-utility reading skill leads into practice of the skill applied to the reading passage. The vocabulary section after each reading proceeds from the broadband approach mentioned earlier. First come exercises in recognizing

---

[1] Norbert Schmitt and Ronald Carter, Introduction to Formulaic Sequences: Acquisition, Processing, and Use, in Norbert Schmitt, ed. (2004), *Formulaic Sequences: Acquisition, Processing, and Use*, John Benjamins.

[2] At corpus.byu.edu/coca/

academic words and placing them in context. Many of the items in this section are from the Academic Word List (AWL); whether from the AWL or not, every "academic word" is important in academic discourse. Then comes a section of multiword vocabulary, focusing on formulaic sequences as described earlier in this introduction.

Discussion

After studying the vocabulary, students are prompted to use it in discussion activities. Finally, Think and Discuss questions at the end of each reading prompt learners to discuss their opinions on the topic of the reading while making connections to their own lives.

Unit Review

The *Unit Review* consists of two parts: Vocabulary Review and Connect the Readings. The first section of the vocabulary review draws together vocabulary of all types into a richly contextualized exercise. Learners then encounter and practice the vocabulary from the unit, strengthening semantic networks and integrating a wide variety of items into their repertoires. The second section of the unit review, Connect the Readings, takes students' critical-thinking skills to a very high level as they analyze both readings and discover similarities/differences, agreement/disagreement, and other concept relationships.

Reading and Vocabulary Focus has been conceived to respect the wide-ranging curiosity and critical-thinking power of contemporary students. Every day these readers encounter a flood of information. They face unprecedented demands to sort the significant from the trivial and to synthesize information. We are delighted to help them do this by offering great readings, engaging skills development, and top-tier vocabulary learning all in an inviting, visually striking form.

Lawrence J. Zwier
Series Consultant

ONE

FOCUS

1. How many countries in the world have you visited? When did you go to these countries?

2. Which countries would you like to visit in the future?

3. Would you like to visit the Arctic or the Antarctic? Why, or why not?

TRAVEL

A man looks at the northern lights near the Arctic Circle sign in the Yukon Territory, Canada.

Academic Vocabulary

to access	a challenge	a goal
a century	essential	particularly

Multiword Vocabulary

about to	to take note
every step of the way	to travel light
to make it	a wake-up call

Reading Preview

(A) Preview. Read the title of Reading 1. Look at the photos on pages 4–7. Then discuss the following questions with a partner or in a small group.

1. Where do you think this journey takes place?

2. Why would anyone want to go to this area of the world?

3. Is this a difficult area to explore? Why or why not?

(B) Topic vocabulary. The following words appear in Reading 1. Look at the words and answer the questions with a partner.

adventure	frightening	travel
blog	journey	tweet
dangerous	terrified	update
explorer		

1. Which words are about going places?

2. Which words are adjectives? What do these words tell you about the reading?

3. Which words are about sending electronic messages?

(C) Predict. What do you think this reading will be about? Discuss each word in Exercise B and predict how it may relate to the reading.

Tourists on the ship Endeavour in Lemaire Channel, Antarctica

How do today's explorers travel? By plane? By boat? How about by bus? Join Andrew Evans as he gets on and off buses to explore Central and South America.

Forty Days
and
Forty Buses

Imagine a place where the sun rises in October and goes down in March. One day is six months of bright, but cold, sunlight. Fourteen million square miles of ice cover this land. This is Antarctica, the coldest, emptiest place on earth. It's not the kind of place you dream of visiting—unless you are travel writer Andrew Evans.

Evans grew up reading about great explorers. His goal was to be a 21st-century explorer. One day he woke up at five o'clock in the morning with an idea. "That's it. I'll take a bus to Antarctica." In addition, he planned to share the adventure with his followers[1] on Twitter.[2] "I want to write the story as it is happening." On New Year's Day, he set off from Washington, D.C.[3] His journey of 10,000 miles (16,093 kilometers) began.

"This is Antarctica, the coldest, emptiest place on earth."

Evans traveled light. His cell phone was the most essential item. He needed his phone to send tweets to his followers and to update his blog on the Internet. It was going to be a challenge to get cell service in all the countries. He also wasn't sure if he could access the Internet everywhere. Luckily, his phone worked well, and he could usually connect to the Internet. During the journey, he sent over 5,000 tweets to his 10,000 followers.

After three days on a bus traveling across the United States, Evans crossed into Mexico. Forty-eight hours and several buses later, he was in Guatemala. Here his journey slowed down. "Guatemalan buses are colorful and full of chickens," he tweeted to his followers, but the roads were often rough. He was amazed that it only cost him $6.50 to cross the whole country. "D.C. taxi drivers, please take note," he tweeted.

When he left Guatemala, he started to travel more quickly. In one day, he crossed four countries. "It started with a 3:00 a.m. wake-up call in El Salvador. I ate breakfast in Honduras, and a late lunch in Nicaragua, and a well-past-midnight dinner at a truck stop in Costa Rica." Every step of the way, he shared his adventures with his followers. "Whatever I'm writing is happening right now," he told them as he got off one bus and got on another.

The last part of his journey was difficult and, at times, dangerous. It was the rainy season. Roads were muddy, particularly in Bolivia. The buses often got stuck. "The driver made us all push the bus," Evans explained. "I got very good at pushing." On his last bus ride in Argentina, he faced his most frightening moment. The bus was

---

[1] *followers:* people who like to read another person's tweets

[2] *Twitter:* an online message system that allows you to send short messages very quickly

[3] *D.C.:* the District of Columbia; the area of Washington, the capital city of the U.S.

A tour bus on the Uyuni Salt Flat, Bolivia

on a ferry[4] crossing the Strait of Magellan. There was a storm. Waves crashed over the side of the ferry and hit the bus. People were crying. They were terrified. "I'm about to die," he tweeted. Fortunately, the ferry, the bus, and Evans arrived safely.

Forty days after his journey began and 40 buses later, Evans stood in Tierra del Fuego. This is where South America ends. Only the ocean and Antarctica were ahead. He got on a boat. Two days later, he achieved his dream. He arrived at Antarctica. "It's like being on another planet," he said. Like the explorers of the past, Evans made it to the end of the world. Unlike past explorers, he made it by bus, tweeting all the way.

7

_____

[4] *ferry:* a boat that carries people and cars across water

READING COMPREHENSION

Big Picture

A Read the following statements. Check (✓) the four statements that express the main ideas of Reading 1.

_____ **1.** Not many people want to visit Antarctica.

_____ **2.** Evans wanted to explore new and exciting places.

_____ **3.** Evans sent hundreds of tweets to his followers.

_____ **4.** Evans used the Internet to share his adventure with his followers.

_____ **5.** It was sometimes a difficult and dangerous journey.

_____ **6.** The bus got stuck on muddy roads in Bolivia because it was the rainy season.

_____ **7.** There was a storm on the Strait of Magellan.

_____ **8.** Evans achieved his goal of being an explorer.

B Read the following statements. Check (✓) the statement that expresses the main idea of the *whole* reading.

_____ **1.** When he was a child, Evans dreamed of going to Antarctica.

_____ **2.** It took Evans 40 days to travel by bus from Washington, D.C., to Antarctica.

_____ **3.** Some parts of Evans's journey were difficult and dangerous.

_____ **4.** Evans shared his bus journey to Antarctica with his online followers.

Close-Up

A Choose the best answer for each of the following questions, according to the reading.

1. Which statement is *not* true, according to paragraph 1?
   a. In Antarctica, the sun shines all day and all night for about six months each year.
   b. The sun shines in Antarctica from October to March.
   c. Many people want to visit this cold and empty place.
   d. Andrew Evans dreamed of visiting Antarctica.

2. Why did Evans send tweets to his online followers?
   a. He enjoyed reading about the adventures of other explorers.
   b. He didn't want his friends and his followers to worry about him.
   c. He couldn't use his phone because cell service was poor.
   d. He wanted to share his exciting adventure as it happened.

3. What worried Evans before he left?
   a. He didn't know if he could get buses from Washington, D.C., to Argentina.
   b. He wasn't sure that he could stay connected with his followers.
   c. He knew roads in the rainy season were muddy.
   d. He worried that the Strait of Magellan was often difficult to cross.

4. Why did his journey slow down in Guatemala?
   a. The roads were very muddy, and the buses often got stuck.
   b. The buses were very crowded.
   c. It was difficult to drive on the rough roads.
   d. Bus drivers in Guatemala drive slowly.

5. Which statement is true, according to paragraphs 6 and 7?
   a. Pushing the bus in Bolivia was Evans's scariest moment.
   b. The storm was so bad that Evans thought he might die on the ferry.
   c. The ferry across the Strait of Magellan took him all the way to Antarctica.
   d. When he got to Tierra del Fuego, he got on his last bus.

B Compare answers to Exercise A with a partner. Then discuss this question:

Do you think traveling by bus is a good way to see a country?

Reading Skill

Understanding Time Order

When authors write about a person's life or an important event, they often organize the information in time order. The reading begins with the first event. It finishes with the last event. Time signals help readers understand time order.

Examples:

at 10:00 a.m.; on May 8; in 2010; from 2014 to 2018

after; before; when; while; until

during this time; one week later; the next year

A Reread paragraphs 2 through 7 of Reading 1. As you read, underline the time signals.

B Circle the correct time signal in each of the following sentences.

1. Evans began his journey (on / in) January 1.

2. Evans arrived in Guatemala about two days (before / after) he was in Mexico.

3. (While / After) he was in Honduras, he had time to eat breakfast.

4. The roads were muddy in Bolivia. (During this time / Several days later), the bus got stuck.

5. Evans arrived in Tierra del Fuego. Two days (before / later), he was in Antarctica.

C Read this paragraph about another explorer to Antarctica, Captain Scott. Complete the sentences with the words in the box.

after	before	during	from	in	later	next	on	to	when

Robert Scott was born _____ June 6th, 1868. He was a British explorer. He wanted
                          1

to be the first person to get to the South Pole in Antarctica. In the weeks _____ he left
                                                                              2

for the South Pole, he made sure he had all his essential items such as food, water, and

warm clothing. _____ 1911, he set off by boat. However, he had to wait several weeks
                   3

for better weather. _____ this time, he planned his journey carefully. Then on
                        4

November 1, 1911, he and his men started the 800-mile walk across the ice. It was a

difficult and dangerous journey. Ten weeks _____, Scott finally reached the South
                                               5

Pole. However, _____ he got there, he saw a flag. Another explorer had arrived
                   6

several days earlier. _____ two days, Scott began the journey back to the boat.
                          7

_____ January _____ March, he walked with his men. It was very cold. The men
   8   **9**

did not have enough food. On March 19, they had to stop again because of bad weather.

The _____ day, the weather got worse. Sadly, Scott and his men never made it back.
       10

VOCABULARY PRACTICE

Academic Vocabulary

A Find the words in the box in Reading 1. Use the paragraph numbers to help you.
Then use the context to help you understand the meaning. Choose the correct word to
complete each of the following sentences.

goal (Par. 2)	essential (Par. 3)	access (Par. 3)
century (Par. 2)	challenge (Par. 3)	particularly (Par. 6)

1. When you travel, it is _____ (very important) to keep your passport and
   money safe.

2. Communicating with people in different countries is a _____ (problem) if you
   do not learn their language.

3. I couldn't _____ (get to) the information because I had no cell service.

4. Abdul's _____ (plan) is to study engineering at the university in Dubai.

5. In the next _____ (100 years), people may not need to carry passports; the information will be electronic.

6. I don't like cold weather, _____ (especially) when it rains all the time.

B Choose the correct word to complete each of the following sentences. Notice and learn the words in bold because they often appear with the academic words.

access	century	challenge	essential	goal	particularly

1. The Internet was probably the most important new technology in the **last** _____.

2. Right now, I just want to pass this class, but my **long-term** _____ is to become a nurse.

3. Learning English today is _____ **important** because we live in a global world.

4. One South Pole explorer said his **greatest** _____ was to make sure that all his men returned home safely.

5. Water is a(n) _____ **item** to take with you on a long walk.

6. If you have a computer and Internet service, you can _____ **information** from libraries all over the world.

Multiword Vocabulary

A Find the multiword vocabulary in bold in Reading 1. Use the paragraph numbers to help you. Use the context to help you understand the meaning. Then match each item to the correct definition.

_____ **1. traveled light** (Par. 3)   **a.** succeeded in something

_____ **2. take note** (Par. 4)   **b.** a morning alarm

_____ **3. wake-up call** (Par. 5)   **c.** each part of a process

_____ **4. every step of the way** (Par. 5)   **d.** going to happen

_____ **5. about to** (Par. 6)   **e.** packed a small amount of clothing

_____ **6. made it** (Par. 7)   **f.** pay attention to something

B Complete the following sentences with the correct multiword vocabulary from Exercise A.

1. I need an early _____ tomorrow morning because my plane leaves at 6:00 a.m.

2. The student was nervous because the test was _____ begin.

3. When I went to Egypt, I _____ because I didn't want to carry a lot of luggage.

4. "_____," said the teacher. "You must hand in your homework tomorrow."

5. The journey across India was very difficult and tiring, but I _____.

6. My driving instructor helped me _____, and I finally passed my test.

Use the Vocabulary

Write answers to the following questions. Use the words in bold in your answers. Then share your answers with a partner.

1. What are your educational **goals** right now? How will you achieve, or be successful in, these goals?

2. When you go on vacation, do you **travel light**, or do you take lots of luggage? Explain your answer.

3. Which subject at school is **particularly** difficult for you? Why? What are you doing to try to better understand this subject?

4. How do you feel when you are **about to** take an important test?

5. Teachers often say reading is an **essential** part of learning English. Do you agree? If so, why do you think reading is so important? If not, what is another way you can improve your English?

6. New students face the **challenge** of making friends. Is this a challenge for you? What does your school or your teacher do to help new students get to know each other?

7. Classrooms are very different today than they were in the **last century**. What do you think are some of the biggest differences?

Andrew Evans

THINK AND DISCUSS

Work in a small group. Use the information in the reading and your own ideas to discuss the following questions.

1. **Summarize.** Describe Evans's journey from Washington, D.C., to Antarctica.

2. **Evaluate.** In the past, explorers discovered new lands. Today, Andrew Evans wants to be a 21st-century explorer. Is it more difficult to be an explorer today than in the past? Explain your answer.

3. **Express an opinion.** Thousands of people read about Evans's adventure on his blog. Why do you think people like to read travel blogs?

Academic Vocabulary

an applicant	to recover	to select
including	a response	to submit

Multiword Vocabulary

to be under a lot of pressure	to hope for the best
to come up with	in short
to have a good time	too good to be true

You visit beautiful beaches. You swim in warm, clear water. You go to fancy hotels and eat in expensive restaurants. Are you on vacation? No, you are working, and it's wonderful!

Reading Preview

A **Preview.** Look at the title of the reading, the photos, and the job description on pages 12–15. Then discuss the following questions with a partner or in a small group.

1. Where exactly is the perfect job?

2. How much money will the job pay?

3. How does a person apply for this job?

B **Topic vocabulary.** The following words appear in Reading 2. Look at the words and answer the questions with a partner.

application	islands	swimming
diving	jet skiing	tourists
hire	resorts	website
interview		

1. What are "tourists"? Which words are about activities or things tourists might do?

2. Which words are about finding and getting a new job?

3. Which words are about places?

C **Predict.** What do you think this reading will be about? Discuss each word in Exercise B and predict how it may relate to the reading.

Perfect Place, Perfect Job

A view from the air of the Great Barrier Reef, Australia.

PERFECT PLACE, PERFECT JOB

Each year, two million tourists visit the beautiful islands off the Australian coast. However, most visitors just visit for a day. The tourism officials wanted more people to stay longer, so they decided to hire a person to live on an island and write about the area. "We are looking for someone to tell the stories of the Great Barrier Reef, and we have come up with what we think is the dream job," explained Anthony Hayes, the Chief Executive of Tourism in Queensland. They posted[1] the job on their website and waited for responses. 1

In England, Ben Southall was looking online. He saw the job posting. It sounded too 2

> "*The interview was unusual: four days of swimming, diving, and writing blogs about the experience.*"

good to be true. He immediately made a video about himself. He loved to travel. He described his 40,000-mile (64,374-kilometer) trip around Africa. He was a good writer and an excellent swimmer, he explained. In short, he was the perfect job applicant. Then he submitted his application and hoped for the best.

Back in Australia, the tourism officials in Queensland were very busy. They received 35,000 applications from people all over the world. They chose 15 top applicants—including Southall. Then they invited these applicants to Australia. The interview was unusual: four days of swimming, diving, and writing blogs about the experience. At the end of the four days, they selected the best applicant: Ben Southall. 3

This was the beginning of Southall's amazing experience. From his first day at work to his 4

---

[1] *posted:* made information available to people on the Internet

Ben Southall on Hamilton Island, Queensland, Australia

THE BEST JOB IN THE WORLD

— WANTED —

A caretaker for the islands on the Great Barrier Reef—full-time with flexible hours.

Salary: US $103,000.00 for 6 months plus free accommodation in a luxury beach house.

If you think you are the ideal person, send us a video and tell us why.

experience: jet skiing, staying in five-star resorts, diving, and then writing about it." Meanwhile, people were reading his blogs all over the world.

It wasn't all fun, however. Australia is home 5 to many poisonous creatures such as snakes, spiders, and fish. For most of the time, Southall managed to avoid these creatures. However, in the last week, his luck came to an end. A poisonous jellyfish stung him. Luckily, he recovered and was able to finish his work.

last, he explored the islands. He swam in the clear, blue water and dived among the coral reefs.[2] He visited local hotels, and he ate at all the best restaurants. "Every day was a different

In the end, was this the perfect job? Yes, but 6 Southall discovered that it was extremely hard work. He was under a lot of pressure to write about all his adventures. He had to post videos and photos every day. These videos and blogs attracted more people to the island. So, Ben Southall swam, dived, had a good time, and did a good job. In fact, he had such a good time that he decided to stay in Australia.

---

[2] *coral reefs:* long narrow areas of coral and rock, just below the ocean surface

READING COMPREHENSION

Big Picture

A Read the following statements. Check (✓) the five statements that express the main ideas of Reading 2.

_____ **1.** Australian tourist officials wanted to get more people to stay on the islands around the Great Barrier Reef.

_____ **2.** Ben Southall believed he had a good chance to get this job.

_____ **3.** A lot of people from many countries wanted this job.

_____ **4.** The Queensland officials interviewed 15 people.

_____ **5.** The successful applicant must be good at swimming, diving, and writing blogs.

_____ **6.** Southall stayed in beautiful hotels on the beach.

_____ **7.** There are poisonous jellyfish in Australia.

_____ **8.** Southall had to work very hard at this job.

B Read the following statements. Check (✓) the statement that expresses the main idea of the *whole* reading.

_____ **1.** Two million tourists visit the Great Barrier Reef islands every year.

_____ **2.** Ben Southall found the perfect job on the Great Barrier Reef.

_____ **3.** The interview for this job was very unusual.

_____ **4.** A lot of people watched Southall's videos and read his blogs.

Close-Up

A Choose the best answer for each of the following questions, according to the reading.

1. Why did Southall believe he was the right person for the job?
   a. He had already traveled thousands of miles across Australia.
   b. He had experience working as a tourism official.
   c. He believed his skills and experience prepared him for the job.
   d. He knew how to make a video about his experience.

2. Which statement is correct?
   a. Applicants had to send a video as part of their application.
   b. People had to call to explain why they wanted this job.
   c. The tourism officials received thousands of applications from England.
   d. About 35,000 people went to Australia to apply for the job.

3. Why was the interview process unusual?
   a. The tourism officials received 35,000 applications.
   b. The applicants had to go to Australia for the interview.
   c. The applicants had to show they could swim and dive.
   d. The tourism officials chose Southall to do the job.

4. Which statement is *not* correct?
   a. Eating at good restaurants was part of Southall's job.
   b. Some of Australia's snakes and fish are poisonous.
   c. Southall managed to keep away from Australia's poisonous creatures.
   d. Southall did not have to pay rent for his beach house.

5. Why did Southall think this job was hard work?
   a. Swimming and diving were tiring.
   b. He was stung by a jellyfish.
   c. He had to visit a lot of hotels and restaurants.
   d. Each day, he had to write and post photos online.

Reading Skill

Finding the Main Idea of a Paragraph

A paragraph is a group of sentences about one main idea. This main idea is the most important idea of the paragraph. The main idea can be in any sentence in a paragraph. You usually need to read the whole paragraph to find the main idea. Finding the main idea of a paragraph will help you understand academic reading.

Ask two questions to find the main idea:

- What is the general subject, or topic, of the paragraph?
- What does the writer say about this topic?

A Read the following paragraph. Then answer the questions below.

Every year, thousands of visitors go to Australia. Many of these visitors worry about Australia's poisonous creatures. They know that the 10 most poisonous snakes in the world live in Australia. Tourism officials say visitors should not worry because these creatures keep away from people. They do not often sting or bite people.

1. What is the general topic of this paragraph?
   a. Visitors to Australia
   b. The 10 most poisonous snakes
   c. Australia's poisonous creatures

2. What is the main idea of the paragraph?
   a. Thousands of people visit Australia every year.
   b. The 10 most poisonous snakes in the world are in Australia.
   c. People do not need to worry about Australia's poisonous creatures.

B Look back at Reading 2 in order to answer the following questions.

1. What is the main idea of paragraph 2?
   a. Southall traveled 40,000 miles around Africa.
   b. Southall had the right kind of experience for this job.
   c. Southall applied for the job by submitting a video.

2. What is the main idea of paragraph 4?
   a. Southall had a wonderful experience.
   b. He swam almost every day.
   c. People all over the world read Southall's blogs

3. What is the main idea of paragraph 5?
   a. There are many dangerous creatures in Australia.
   b. Southall recovered from a poisonous jellyfish sting.
   c. Southall was unlucky while he was swimming.

VOCABULARY PRACTICE

Academic Vocabulary

A Find the words in bold in Reading 2. Use the paragraph numbers to help you. Then use the context and the sentences below to help you choose the correct definition.

1. The teacher's **responses** (Par. 1) to the student's question were not very helpful. The student didn't understand what she said, so he asked her for more information.
   a. grades   b. answers

2. Peter **submitted** (Par. 2) his report on the first Monday of the month.
   a. checked   b. sent in

3. The company chose several people—**including** (Par. 3) me—to go to the meeting in Paris. I was excited about the trip because I had never been to Paris.
   a. one of them was   b. but not

4. After the interviews, the manager told the **applicants** (Par. 3) that she would make her decision the following day.
   a. people who work for a company   b. people who are trying to get a new job

5. Last month, the travel magazine **selected** (Par. 3) the best photos that travelers sent in. Then they put the photos in the magazine for everyone to see.

    a. chose   **b.** discussed

6. After I **recovered** (Par. 5) from the accident, I was able to go back to work again.

    a. was injured   **b.** got better

B Choose the correct word to complete each of the following sentences. Notice and learn the words in bold because they often appear with the academic words.

applicant	including	recovered	response	selected	submit

1. After the student _____ **from a serious illness**, she was able to go back to school.

2. Janet Lee got the job because she was clearly **the most qualified** _____ .

3. Please _____ **your application** online—do not mail in this information.

4. The manager _____ **a team** of experienced employees to travel with him to Seoul.

5. This is a serious problem, and we need a **quick** _____ .

6. The manager asked me for personal information _____ **my phone number and email address**.

Multiword Vocabulary

A Find the multiword vocabulary in bold in Reading 2. Use the paragraph numbers to help you. Use the context to help you understand the meaning. The match each item to the correct definition.

_____ **1. come up with** (Par. 1)

_____ **2. too good to be true** (Par. 2)

_____ **3. in short** (Par. 2)

_____ **4. hoped for the best** (Par. 2)

_____ **5. was under a lot of pressure** (Par. 6)

_____ **6. had a good time** (Par. 6)

a. felt stressed and worried about doing something

b. to say in a few words

c. enjoyed yourself

d. think of a new idea

e. thinking something is so fantastic that there might be something wrong

f. wanted everything to happen in a good way

B Complete the following paragraph with the correct multiword vocabulary from Exercise A.

I often read travel blogs because I love to travel. Last year, I read about a competition. People had to write about why travel is important. The best story won a free trip to Thailand! It seemed

_____. So I quickly thought about the question. I tried to

1

_____ some good ideas. I uploaded some photos from earlier

2

trips. After I submitted the application, I waited and _____.

                                                      3

However, a few weeks later, I heard that I didn't win. I was disappointed because I really wanted

to go on a trip. I _____ at work, and I needed a vacation. So I

                                       4

decided to visit my friend who lives just 50 miles away from my home. We

_____—even though it was not Thailand!

5

_____, you don't have to go far to enjoy traveling.

6

Use the Vocabulary

Write answers to the following questions. Use the words in bold in your answers. Then share your answers with a partner.

1. Parents often want their children to go to very good universities. Sometimes this means high school students **are under a lot of pressure**. Do you think students can do well if they **are under a lot of pressure**? Explain your answer.

2. When have you taken a difficult test and **hoped for the best**? What happened?

3. In most countries, high school students have to **submit** their grades when they apply to a college or university. Some schools also ask you to write a letter explaining why they should **select** you. Think of a country you know well. What information do students have to **submit** with an application?

4. Imagine you are in a math class. You don't understand an important part of the lesson. When you ask the teacher for help, his **response** is disappointing. He tells you to figure it out by yourself. What would you do in this situation?

5. Someone calls you on the phone. She says she is calling from your bank. She wants personal information, **including** your bank account number. What would you tell her?

THINK AND DISCUSS

Work in a small group. Use the information in the reading and your own ideas to discuss the following questions.

1. **Evaluate.** Why do you think the Australian tourism officials chose Southall for this job?

2. **Analyze.** Do you think they were happy with Southall's work? Why, or why not?

3. **Express an opinion.** This job was only for six months. Do you think this job helped Southall get another job? How?

Vocabulary Review

A Complete the paragraphs with the vocabulary below that you have studied in the unit.

about to	last century
came up with	long-term goal
every step of the way	made it
greatest challenge	recovered from his illness

You may think that all great adventures happened in the _____ . Ed Stafford believes
1
there are still adventures today. One day, Stafford was online. He was reading about the Amazon River, the longest river in the world. He

_____ a great idea. No one had
2
ever walked from the beginning to the end of this river. Stafford decided he would become the first person to do this.

Ed Stafford on his journey down the Amazon

On April 2, 2008, Stafford set out on his 4,000-mile walk. The jungle was hot, frightening, and dangerous. During the journey, he met a local man who then

walked with him _____ . This was particularly useful because this man
3
helped him communicate with local people. After 14 months of walking, however, Stafford had no

more money. He had to catch fish to live. Sometimes he was _____ give up
4
because he was so hungry. He also got sick, but when he _____ , he continued
5
his journey. Finally, 860 days after he started, Stafford _____ to the end of the
6
river. He later described it as the _____ of his life. Now he has a new
7
_____ : to find an even more challenging adventure for the future.
8

B Compare answers to Exercise A with a partner. Then discuss the following question.

What do you think was the most difficult part of Stafford's journey?

C Complete the following sentences in a way that shows that you understand the meaning of the words in bold.

1. I think it is **particularly important** for teachers to _____ .

2. The following are **essential items** to take with you while you are traveling in a different country:

_____ .

3. It is better to **travel light** because _____ .

4. Juan lost everything in his wallet **including** his _____ .

D Work with a partner and write four sentences that include any four of the vocabulary items below. You may use any verb tense and make nouns plural if you want.

access information	have a good time	the most qualified applicant
be under a lot of pressure	hope for the best	a wake-up call

Connect the Readings

A Use information from Reading 1 and Reading 2 to answer the following questions.

1. Evans and Southall both traveled to exciting, but different places. In what ways were their journeys different? Answer the questions below. Then add three more questions and fill in the chart.

Differences	Andrew Evans	Ben Southall
Where did they leave from?		
Where did they go?		

2. What are some similarities between the two men and their adventures? Make a list of these similarities.

_____

_____

_____

_____

B With a partner or in a small group, compare answers to Exercise A. Then discuss the following questions about Andrew Evans and Ben Southall.

1. Which man had the most difficult adventure? Why?

2. Who prepared the most carefully for his adventure?

3. Evans and Southall had very different adventures. What do you think was the biggest difference?

C Discuss the following questions with a partner. Use your understanding of the readings and your own ideas.

1. Do you agree that Evans is a real explorer?

2. Are there any parts of the world where people can still explore today?

3. Some people say that the next place to explore is space. Do you think we will see many space explorers this century? Where will they explore? How will they get there?

FIRE
AND
WATER

A man quickly turns burning wool round and round over water to create a work of art.

FOCUS

1. Fire and water can be both beautiful and dangerous. When is fire dangerous? When is water dangerous?

2. What can cause a fire to start?

3. What damage can water cause?

Academic Vocabulary

a decade	an increase	a policy
an expert	an individual	a role

Multiword Vocabulary

as a result	on average
to get rid of	to set something on fire
in the past	to share a common bond

Reading Preview

A Preview. Read the first sentence of each paragraph on pages 26–28. Check (✓) each topic you think will be in Reading 1.

_____ **1.** The growing number of wildfires

_____ **2.** Reasons why house fires begin

_____ **3.** How people put out, or stopped, fires in the past

_____ **4.** The connection between hotter weather and fires

_____ **5.** Why fires are a part of nature

_____ **6.** How much fires cost to put out

B Topic vocabulary. The following words appear in Reading 1. Look at the words and answer the questions with a partner.

climate	forest	threat
damage	lightning	vegetation
deadly	risk	wildfire
destroy	temperatures	wind

1. What is a "wildfire"? Which word or words tell you where or how a wildfire might happen?

2. Which words are about the weather?

3. A wildfire can be very dangerous. Which words relate to danger?

C Predict. What do you think this reading will be about? Discuss each word in Exercise B and predict how it may relate to the reading.

The forest is on fire! Trees are burning! The fire is going to destroy this forest. Or will it? Read about why fire can sometimes be good for a forest.

A wildfire burns close to a road in Bastrop State Park, Texas, USA.

Nature's Fires

High in the Russian sky, a young man stands at the airplane door. The forest below is burning. He takes a deep breath and jumps into the thick smoke. A woman walks through a dry forest in the United States. As she walks, she sets the grass on fire. In southern Australia, a pilot flies low over burning trees. He drops a huge amount of water onto the flames below. These are three different individuals, in three different situations and countries. Yet they share a common bond: They are risking their lives to put out wildfires.

There have always been wildfires. However, today there are many more fires than in previous

At a wildfire in Montana, USA, a firefighter radios to fire crews.

WHAT ABOUT THE ANIMALS?

In a wildfire, people are not the only ones to lose their homes. Animals lose their homes, too. People can usually get into a car and escape the flames. But what about the animals? How do they escape? According to one wildfire expert, we should not be too concerned. "Don't worry about the animals," says Bill Leenhouts. "Most animals actually escape the fires." And when the fire is over, the wildlife begins to return. First, the insects come back. Then the birds return to feed on these insects. As new vegetation begins to grow, plant-eating animals move back. And finally meat-eating animals return, too. Wildfires even help the returning animals. Burned holes in trees provide perfect new homes for the returning wildlife.

decades. Over 100,000 wildfires burn each year in the United States. Russia has 20,000 to 35,000 wildfires annually. Australia has on average 60,000 each year. These fires destroy huge areas of forest and burn hundreds of homes. They cause millions of dollars in damage and, unfortunately, are often deadly.

Many experts believe there are several 3 reasons for this sudden increase in wildfires. The first reason is climate change.[1] Recent weather has been warmer and drier than in the past. This leads to dangerous fire conditions. When lightning strikes, dry grass easily catches fire. Hot winds add to the problem. The wind spreads a fire quickly, up to 14 miles per hour (23 kilometers per hour) in some cases. In 2010,

---

[1] *climate change:* changes in the Earth's weather over a long period of time

Russia had the hottest and driest summer in a century. Heat, lightning, and wind were a disastrous combination. Fires burned out of control. In just one month, 500 fires destroyed over 2,000 homes. Some people lost their lives.

Traditional fire-fighting practices are another reason for the increase in fires. In the United States, firefighters used to quickly put out every fire. They didn't allow the grass and trees to burn. As a result, today many forests have thicker vegetation. Thicker vegetation means more fuel for fires. Also, without fires from time to time, forests become overcrowded and unhealthy. Insects such as the bark beetle move in and kill the trees. The dead wood then easily catches fire. So, surprisingly, the United States has many more fires today partly because of its past fire-fighting practices.

Scientists now understand that a fire can be a natural part of a healthy forest. As a result, countries like Australia allow more fires to burn naturally. Sometimes, firefighters even start fires to get rid of dead wood. Of course, they carefully control these fires. The fire thins out old trees. This allows sunlight to reach the ground. As a result, fires help new trees to grow.

Many experts predict that higher temperatures will lead to more wildfires. Yet science is changing the way people think about wildfires. More people understand that fire plays an important role in nature. Firefighters will still risk their lives to put out some fires. However, if a fire is not a serious threat to people, firefighters often let it burn naturally. As one firefighter in California says, "We can't let all fires burn, but we can't put out all fires."

READING COMPREHENSION

Big Picture

Ⓐ The following statements are the main ideas of each paragraph in Reading 1. Write the correct paragraph number next to its main idea.

_____ **1.** Climate change is one reason why there are more wildfires today than in the past.

_____ **2.** In the future, firefighters will allow more wildfires to burn naturally.

_____ **3.** Firefighters around the world risk their lives to stop fires.

_____ **4.** There are more wildfires around the world today than in the past.

_____ **5.** One reason there are more forest fires today is that in the past, firefighters always put out every fire.

_____ **6.** Natural fires are part of a healthy forest.

B Read the following statements. Check (✓) the statement that best expresses the main idea of the *whole* reading.

_____ **1.** Each year, wildfires cause millions of dollars in damage.

_____ **2.** Today there are more wildfires because of climate change.

_____ **3.** The number of wildfires is increasing for several reasons.

_____ **4.** In the future, firefighters will let some wildfires burn.

Close-Up

Choose the answer that best completes each of the following sentences.

1. There are more wildfires _____.
   a. in Australia than there are in the United States
   b. today than there were in the past
   c. in Russia than there are in Australia
   d. in California than in any other part of the United States

2. The Russian fires of 2010 spread very quickly because _____.
   a. the fires burned many homes
   b. lightning spread the fire
   c. the weather was unusually hot, dry, and windy
   d. firefighters could not save every home

3. Because of the traditional fire policy in the United States, _____.
   a. there were fewer wildfires
   b. animals and birds could escape the fires
   c. the weather became warmer and drier
   d. trees and grass became thicker

4. Firefighters in Australia decide to let some wildfires burn because _____.
   a. there are too many wildfires
   b. there are not enough firefighters
   c. the wildfires are too difficult to put out
   d. wildfires can help a forest stay healthy

5. In the future, firefighters _____.
   a. will put out more wildfires because they know how to control them
   b. will see fewer wildfires because of climate change
   c. will allow more wildfires to burn naturally
   d. will not fight any forest fires in California

6. According to the short extra reading, "What about the Animals?," on page 27, _____.
   a. wildlife is often seriously hurt or killed in forest fires
   b. most wildlife can escape a fire and return safely when it is over
   c. birds are the first creatures to return after a forest fire
   d. a forest fire destroys vegetation, so wildlife cannot return for a long time

Reading Skill

Identifying Main Ideas and Supporting Details

A paragraph usually has one main idea. The other sentences in the paragraph contain supporting details. Supporting details are facts (e.g., names and numbers), reasons, and examples that support the main idea. As you read academic information, it is a good idea to take notes of the main idea and the supporting details. This helps you check your understanding and remember the information. Read the following notes from paragraph 2 of the reading.

Main idea:	*Supporting details:*
There are more fires today than in the past.	U.S: 100,000 fires each year
	Russia: 20,000–35,000 fires
	Australia: 60,000 fires

Ⓐ Read the following paragraphs and the statements that follow. Write *MI* if the statement is a main idea. Write *SD* if the statement is a supporting detail.

1. In the United States, lightning and dry conditions start many forest fires. However, people start most forest fires. Someone may throw away a cigarette and it begins to burn dry grass. A family may light a small campfire and forget to put it out. Fires started by humans begin small, but spread very quickly. Four out of five wildfires begin this way.

   _____ **a.** A cigarette can start a fire.

   _____ **b.** Humans start most forest fires in the United States.

   _____ **c.** Fires started by humans can quickly spread and be very dangerous.

2. Fighting wildfires is hard work. Many fires are in mountains. There are often no roads in these areas, so firefighters have to walk long distances to the fire. They carry heavy backpacks. When they get to the fire, they work hard to put it out. It is hot and difficult work. At the end of their day, they often have to walk several miles back to their camp.

   _____ **a.** It is hard and tiring work to fight wildfires.

   _____ **b.** Firefighters must walk long distances at the beginning and end of each day.

   _____ **c.** Firefighters carry heavy bags.

3. All firefighting is dangerous. However, sometimes a wildfire is too dangerous for firefighters. When a wildfire is very dangerous, airplanes fight it from the air. Planes drop huge amounts of water from above. They also drop special chemicals that put out fires.

   _____ **a.** Firefighters use planes to put out very dangerous fires.

   _____ **b.** Planes drop water and chemicals on wildfires.

   _____ **c.** Sometimes wildfires are too dangerous for firefighters on the ground.

B Find two details from Reading 1 to support each of the main ideas. Write them in the chart.

Main Idea	Supporting Details
Hot, dry weather can lead to forest fires.	• _____ • _____
Thick forests can result in more fires.	• _____ • _____

VOCABULARY PRACTICE

Academic Vocabulary

A Find the words in bold in Reading 1. Use the context and the sentences below to help you match each word to its correct definition.

_____ **1.** A team of firefighters consists of several men and women. **Individuals** (Par. 1) may have different ideas, but they all work together on their team.

_____ **2.** The last two **decades** (Par. 2) of the 20th century were the hottest in 400 years. As a result, the number of wildfires increased during this time.

_____ **3.** The fires in Russia were so difficult to put out that the government called in a team of **experts** (Par. 3) to help them.

_____ **4.** There has been an **increase** (Par. 3) in the number of people who live in forest areas. Unfortunately, when there are more people, there are more fires.

_____ **5.** The old **policy** (Par. 4) of putting out all fires has changed. Now firefighters allow some wildfires to burn, especially if there is no risk to people or homes.

_____ **6.** Strong winds played a big **role** (Par. 6) in spreading the forest fire.

a. 10-year periods

b. an official plan or way of doing something

c. a rise

d. a part

e. people

f. people who know a lot about a particular subject

B The words in bold often appear with the words on the left. Find the words in bold in Reading 1. Circle the words that appear with them in the reading.

1. each / different   **individual(s)** (Par. 1)

2. previous / next / first   **decades** (Par. 2)

3. well-known / many / international   **experts** (Par. 3)

4. small / sudden   **increase** (Par. 3)

5. government / strict / fire   **policy** (Par. 4)

6. important / small   **role** (Par. 6)

C Choose a word from the left column in Exercise B to complete each of the following sentences.

1. The teacher has a(n) _____ **policy** that students cannot bring drinks or food into the computer lab, even during lunchtime.

2. What will be the new technology in the _____ **decade**? We can't predict the future, but I'm sure the technology will be exciting.

3. My father is a(n) _____ **expert** in this country, but people in other countries do not know about his work.

4. _____ **individual** is responsible for his or her decisions.

5. This year, there has only been a(n) _____ **increase** in the cost of gas. It costs almost the same as it did 12 months ago.

6. In most countries, the government plays a(n) _____ **role** in educating its citizens.

Multiword Vocabulary

A Find the multiword vocabulary in bold in Reading 1. Use the context to help you understand the meaning. Then match each item to the correct definition.

_____ 1. **sets** the grass **on fire** (Par. 1)   **a.** many years ago

_____ 2. **share a common bond** (Par. 1)   **b.** throw away

_____ 3. **on average** (Par. 2)   **c.** therefore

_____ 4. **in the past** (Par. 3)   **d.** starts a fire

_____ 5. **as a result** (Par. 4)   **e.** normally

_____ 6. **get rid of** (Par. 5)   **f.** are similar in one way

B Complete the following sentences with the correct multiword vocabulary from Exercise A.

1. People understand more about wildfires today than they did _____.

2. _____, a forest firefighter in the United States earns about $41,000 per year.

3. Some people choose to _____ dead grass and old trees near their homes by carefully burning them.

4. Temperatures are increasing in many parts of the world. _____, experts believe there will be more fires in the future because the weather will be hotter and drier.

5. A firefighter sometimes fights fire with fire. He or she carefully _____ to make sure it will not burn in the future.

6. Firefighters in Russia and Australia may speak different languages, but they _____: They risk their lives to put out fires.

Use the Vocabulary

Complete the following sentences with your own ideas. Then share your answers with a partner.

1. Many people in the western United States build their homes out of wood. **As a result**, these homes

   _____.

2. If you want to **get rid of** an old computer, you should _____.

3. Police officers and firefighters **share a common bond**: They both _____.

4. **In the past**, people didn't use _____.

5. **On average**, about 90 percent of students _____.

6. The boy accidently **set** the grass **on fire** when he _____.

7. In the **next decade**, people will be able to _____.

8. Garbage is becoming a serious problem in many cities, so I think **each individual** should

   _____.

THINK AND DISCUSS

Work in a small group. Use the information in the reading and your own ideas to discuss the following questions.

1. **Summarize.** According to Reading 1, why are there more wildfires today than in past decades? Have you seen more fires in the area where you live?

2. **Apply information.** Some wildfires are natural. Does this mean we cannot prevent wildfires from happening? Is it possible for people to reduce the number of fires in the future?

3. **Express an opinion.** In some parts of the United States, people move away from busy cities. They build homes in forests. The government often warns these people about the danger of wildfires. Yet they still build. If there is a fire, do you think the firefighters should always try to save these homes? Or should they allow some fires to burn naturally as Reading 1 describes?

Imagine every year that water destroys your house and you lose everything. What would you do? Find out about how the people of Bangladesh live with these floods.

Academic Vocabulary

a community	a majority	to survive
to experience	normal	a system

Multiword Vocabulary

above sea level   no longer

to face many   to wash away
    challenges   the worst-case scenario

in fact

Reading Preview

A **Preview.** Look at the photos on pages 34–37. Then discuss the following questions with a partner or in a small group.

1. Look at the map on page 37. A large part of Bangladesh is colored blue. What does this mean?

2. Why do you think Bangladesh experiences floods? Use the map and the photo to help you.

3. There are many farmers in Bangladesh. How does flooding affect these farmers?

4. Are there floods where you live? Have you ever experienced a flood?

B **Topic vocabulary.** The following words appear in Reading 2. Look at the words and answer the questions with a partner.

coastal	flood	rivers
crops	overcrowded	seafood
disaster	rice	seawater
farmers		

1. Bangladesh is a country near northeastern India. Which words tell you about how people may live in this country?

2. Which words show that life is sometimes difficult in this country?

3. Which words are about water?

C **Predict.** What do you think this reading will be about? Discuss each word in Exercise B and predict how it may relate to the reading.

A Wall of Water

A woman and her child sit inside their flooded home in Kurigram, Bangladesh.

The Brahmaputra River floods farmland in Bangladesh.

At ten o'clock on the morning of May 25, 2009, Nasir Uddin was standing outside his mud house. He noticed that the river next to his house was higher than normal. He looked toward the sea. He suddenly saw a huge wall of brown water. It was rushing toward him. Within minutes, the water came into his house. It washed away the mud walls. Uddin and his three young daughters jumped onto the kitchen table. "I was sure we were all dead," he later said. Incredibly, an empty boat passed by. He managed to put his daughters in the boat. He held on to its side. This Bangladeshi family was fortunate. They survived this disaster, but hundreds of their neighbors died.

Floods happen when a river or the sea rises and covers dry land. Unfortunately, Bangladesh often experiences floods. This is because the majority of its land is less than 15 feet (5 meters) above sea level. The sea level is rising because of global warming.[1] As it rises, it covers more land in Bangladesh. In the worst-case scenario, the country may lose one quarter of its land by the end of the century. This is very serious because millions of people live close to the sea.

Coastal flooding is also very destructive because it covers the land with salty seawater. The salt stays in the soil even after the flood is over. When there is too much salt, farmers cannot grow their crops. This is happening to farming communities in Bangladesh. Frequent coastal flooding is destroying farms and crops. As a result, many farmers can no longer farm. Unfortunately, farmers often have nowhere to go. They cannot move to a new area because Bangladesh is so overcrowded. In fact, it is one of the most crowded countries in the world.

Bangladeshis face many challenges from flooding. Yet this is a nation of strong people. They are finding solutions. Bangladeshi farmers now grow special rice in salt water. They raise seafood such as shrimp and crab in areas closest to the sea. In addition, they have built huge walls of earth. They hope these walls will keep the sea away from their vegetable farms. They have also built shelters[2] and developed an early-warning system. "Let me tell you about Bangladeshis," says Zakir Kibria, a farming expert. "We may be poor . . . , but we are not victims."

So, when Uddin lost his home that day, he did what most Bangladeshis do: He rebuilt. This time, however, he built his house out of wood, not mud. He wants his home to survive the next flood.

---

[1] *global warming:* an increase in the Earth's average temperature over a long period of time

[2] *shelters:* special buildings where people go to have protection from dangerous weather

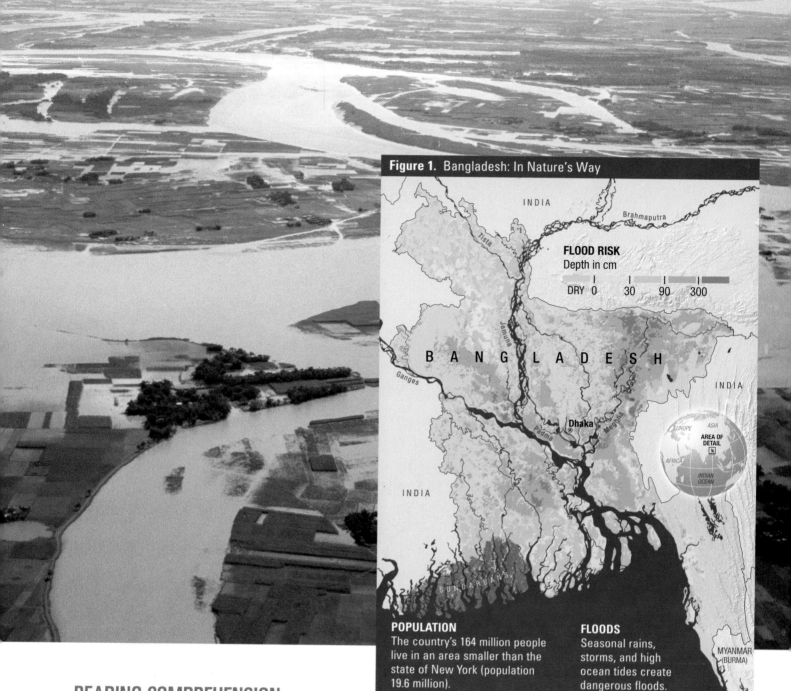

Figure 1. Bangladesh: In Nature's Way

FLOOD RISK
Depth in cm

DRY 0   30   90   300

BANGLADESH

INDIA

Brahmaputra

Tista

Jamuna

Ganges

Padma

Dhaka

Meghna

INDIA

INDIA

SUNDARBANS

MYANMAR (BURMA)

AREA OF DETAIL

EUROPE ASIA
AFRICA
INDIAN OCEAN

POPULATION
The country's 164 million people live in an area smaller than the state of New York (population 19.6 million).

FLOODS
Seasonal rains, storms, and high ocean tides create dangerous floods.

Source: National Geographic Magazine, May 2011

READING COMPREHENSION

Big Picture

Choose the answer that best completes each of the following sentences.

1. The main idea of the whole reading is that _____.
   a. coastal flooding can be very serious
   b. flooding is a serious problem in Bangladesh
   c. global warming is leading to serious flooding in some parts of the world

2. This reading begins with the story of Uddin because _____.
   a. Uddin and his family were lucky to survive the flood
   b. Uddin managed to save his family
   c. Uddin's experience shows the danger of floods

3. The main idea of paragraph 2 is that _____.
   a. in Bangladesh, floods are a serious problem
   b. millions of people in Bangladesh live close to the sea
   c. in the future, the country might lose 25 percent of its land

4. The two biggest challenges for Bangladeshi farmers are _____.
   a. salty soil; not enough land
   b. raising seafood; rising sea levels
   c. growing special rice; building shelters

5. The main idea of paragraph 4 is that _____.
   a. Bangladeshi farmers are building seawalls and raising shrimp and crab
   b. Bangladeshi farmers are finding solutions to the problem of serious flooding
   c. Bangladeshis are not victims

Close-Up

Ⓐ Decide which of the following statements are true or false, according to the reading. Write *T* (True) or *F* (False) next to each one.

_____ 1. Uddin ran out of his house when he saw the huge wall of water.

_____ 2. Many of Uddin's neighbors did not survive the flood.

_____ 3. Most of Bangladesh is 15 feet or more above sea level.

_____ 4. Climate change is one reason why Bangladesh floods.

_____ 5. In 2100, Bangladesh may have 25 percent less land because of flooding.

_____ 6. Farmers there grow rice and raise seafood behind huge walls that keep the sea away from farms.

_____ 7. Kibria believes his country will find solutions to the problem of floods.

_____ 8. Uddin built his new house in exactly the same way as his old house.

Ⓑ Work with a partner or in a small group. Change the false sentences in Exercise A to make them true.

Reading Skill

Identifying Cause and Effect

In academic readings, writers often explain why something happens (a cause) and what happens as a result (an effect).

Sometimes a signal word introduces cause and effect. *Because* introduces a cause.

  Because of the rain, the river flooded.

As a result and *so* introduce effects.

  It rained, *so* the river flooded.

Other times, the general context helps you figure out causes and effects.

A Match each cause to its effect.

Cause

_____ **1.** Uddin built a new home made of wood.

_____ **2.** Bangladesh is very overcrowded.

_____ **3.** There is a lot of salt in the ground.

Effect

a. Farmers can no longer grow some crops.

b. He hopes the house will float in the next flood.

c. Farmers cannot move away from the sea and find new land.

B Reread Reading 2. Write one effect for each of these causes.

Cause

1. Uddin put his children in a boat.

2. The farmers built huge seawalls.

3. The farms closest to the sea are very salty.

Effect

_____

_____

_____

VOCABULARY PRACTICE

Academic Vocabulary

A Read the following sentences. Underline the word or words in the second sentence that mean the same as the word in bold in the first sentence. The first one is done for you.

1. For the last few days, the weather has been hotter than **normal**. The usual temperature at this time of year is about 70 degrees Fahrenheit. However, it has been over 100 degrees all week

2. Some people **survived** the flood by climbing onto their roofs. Other people stayed alive by leaving the city before the storm came.

3. The southern part of the United States often **experiences** storms and floods. Other areas have only a little rainfall and are very dry.

4. When they heard the storm was going to be bad, the **majority** of people left. Most of them went to the homes of family and friends who lived in a safer place.

5. The government told all the **communities** to prepare for bad weather. As a result, a lot of people in the area bought extra food and water and stayed inside.

6. We need a new computer **system**. The way things work right now is not good enough. For example, the computers are very slow.

B The words in bold often appear with the words on the right. Find the words in bold in Reading 2. Circle the word or words that appear with them in the reading.

1. _____ **normal** (Par. 1)   less rain than / higher than

2. **survived** _____ (Par. 1)   this disaster / the accident

3. **experiences** _____ (Par. 2)   difficulties / floods

4. **majority** _____ (Par. 2)   of people / of its land

5. _____ **communities** (Par. 3)   international / local / farming

6. _____ **system** (Par. 4)   early-warning / new

C Choose a word or phrase from the right column in Exercise B to complete each of the following sentences.

1. I wanted to study art, but I was worried that I would **experience** _____ in finding a job, so I switched to computer design.

2. The _____ **communities** near my home all wanted the government to build a new highway to reduce traffic problems.

3. There was _____ **normal**; the water levels in the lakes and rivers were very low.

4. The **majority** _____ agree that smoking should not be allowed in or around restaurants.

5. I like the _____ **system** at work: We can sometimes work from home if we have permission from our supervisor.

6. The storm was so strong that it damaged a large part of the city. Many people **survived** _____ by staying in their basements.

Multiword Vocabulary

A Find the multiword vocabulary in bold in Reading 2. Use the context to help you complete each definition.

1. If water **washed away** (Par. 1) an object, it means that the object was _____.
   a. lost
   b. very clean

2. We use the phrase **above sea level** (Par. 2) to describe _____.
   a. the height of the land compared to the sea
   b. how far the land is from the sea

3. When we use the phrase **the worst-case scenario** (Par. 2), we are talking about _____.
   a. the most serious situation that might happen
   b. a bad storm

4. **No longer** (Par. 3) means the same as _____.
   a. something is shorter than it used to be
   b. something used to be the case, but is not now

5. We use **in fact** (Par. 3) in a sentence _____.
   a. to emphasize an important point
   b. to introduce a contrast word

6. When people **face many challenges** (Par. 4), they _____.
   a. question the truth of something
   b. experience difficult situations

B Complete the following paragraphs with the correct multiword vocabulary from the box.

above sea level	in fact	the worst-case scenario
faces many challenges	no longer	washed away

Every year, many people visit Venice in Italy. People call this famous city the City of Water. Often, however, there is too much water. The city is built only a few feet _____ . So when the sea level rises, flooding is very destructive

_____
1

here. In November 2010, for example, the water rose quickly and covered over 70 percent of the city. Water _____ cars and damaged many of its oldest
2
buildings. Residents could _____ get around the city.
3
　　Like other cities, Venice _____ today. Yet floods are the most
4
serious problem. City leaders know that in _____, floods might
5
destroy the city in the future. Everyone worries that global warming will increase the number of floods in the next few decades. _____, the flood of 2010 was one
6
of the worst in the last decades. So experts and city leaders in Venice are trying to find a solution to this problem. They want to find a way to save this beautiful city.

Use the Vocabulary

Write answers to the following questions. Use the words in bold in your answers. Then share your answers with a partner.

1. International students **face many challenges**. Give some examples.
2. When people live in a new country, they often **experience** a different way of life. Do you think this is a good thing?
3. What do the **majority** of students in your class want to do when they graduate from school or college?
4. What grading **system** does your teacher use?
5. What's the **normal** weather where you live?
6. If your area is hit by a big storm, what four things could help you **survive the disaster** for several days?
7. A **community** can refer to people and places connected to where you live. Describe your **local community**. Do you enjoy it, or would you prefer to live in a different kind of community?
8. Can you think of any bad habits that you **no longer** have? For example, did you use to chew your fingernails?

THINK AND DISCUSS

Work in a small group. Use the information in the reading and your own ideas to discuss the following questions.

1. **Identify problems.** What challenges are facing the farmers of Bangladesh?
2. **Identify solutions.** What are these farmers doing to try to solve these challenges?
3. **Relate to personal experience.** Many communities have plans to help people if there is a serious storm. What kind of plans does your community have?

Vocabulary Review

A Complete the paragraphs with the vocabulary below that you have studied in the unit.

faced another challenge	first decade	less rain than normal	washed away
farm communities	in fact	survived this disaster	worst-case scenario

People in Australia call the _____ 1 of the 21st century "The Big Dry." During this time, there was _____ 2 . _____ 3 , some areas had no rain at all. The land was very dry. Then in 2009, the _____ 4 happened. Fires started. These fires quickly spread and destroyed whole towns. Almost 200 people died. It was a terrible time for the people of Australia. To make it even worse, experts found that people started these fires, not lightning.

Incredibly, two years later, the same area _____ 5 : this time, floods. Storm after storm brought heavy rain. As a result, rivers quickly rose and soon a wall of water rushed across the southern part of Australia. The water covered an area larger than France and Germany. It _____ 6 hundreds of homes and damaged both city and _____ 7 . People _____ 8 by leaving their homes and going to higher areas.

B Compare answers to Exercise A with a partner. Then discuss the following questions.

What two reasons explain why fires began at this time in Australia? Do you think the floods two years later were caused by people or by nature?

C Complete the following sentences in a way that shows that you understand the meaning of the words in bold.

1. Many students **experience difficulties** when they _____ .

2. There was a **sudden increase** in the cost of gas because _____ .

3. When Lee lost his job, he was **no longer** able to _____ .

4. I **share a common bond** with my best friend: We both _____ .

A flooded street in Queensland, Australia, January 2011

D Work with a partner and write four sentences that include any four of the vocabulary items below. You may use any verb tense and make nouns plural if you want.

as a result	get rid of	the majority of people
each individual	in the past	many experts

Connect the Readings

A Use information from Reading 1 and Reading 2 to fill in the graphic organizer below.

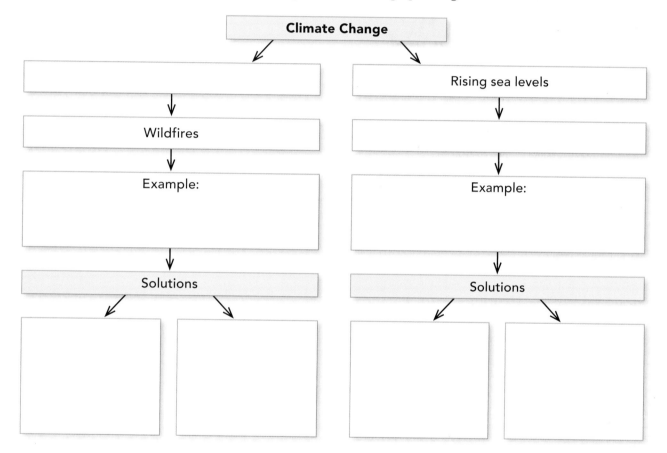

B Reread the text in Vocabulary Review, Exercise A. Underline the main ideas and supporting details. Create a graphic organizer for your underlined information.

C With a partner or in a small group, compare answers to Exercise A. Then discuss the following questions.

1. What are some of the effects of climate change?

2. Which solutions do you think are the best?

D Discuss the following questions with a partner. Use your understanding of the readings and your own ideas.

1. How does climate change cause wildfires? How does it cause floods?

2. Does your country experience wildfires or floods? What can people do to protect themselves from these terrible events?

THREE

The Power of
IDEAS

Mirrors capture sunlight
at an electric power
station in Seville, Spain.

FOCUS

1. What is solar energy, and why do we call it "clean energy"?

2. What are other sources of clean energy?

3. What products do you know that use clean energy?

45

Academic Vocabulary

to encourage	an impact	rural
to estimate	materials	a volunteer

Multiword Vocabulary

basic needs	to give up
to drop out of school	instead of
an elementary school	to keep the cost down

A woman carries a solar light in Iringa, Tanzania.

Reading Preview

A Preview. Read the title and the first sentence of each paragraph in Reading 1. Check (✓) each topic you think will be in the reading. Then discuss your ideas with a partner or in a small group.

_____ **1.** Wadongo's life as a child

_____ **2.** The history of Kenya

_____ **3.** Wadongo's health

_____ **4.** The cost of solar lamps

_____ **5.** Learning English in Kenya

_____ **6.** The use of cell phones in Kenya

B Topic vocabulary. The following words appear in Reading 1. Look at the words and answer the questions with a partner.

communities	grateful	recycled
concerned	lamp	solar
electricity	organization	villagers
frustrated		

1. Which words describe how people feel?

2. Which words most closely relate to light?

3. Which words refer to groups of people?

C Predict. What do you think this reading will be about? Discuss each word in Exercise B and predict how it may relate to the reading.

It's late—time to do your homework. You turn on the light and get started. But what if you had no electricity? Meet one person who has found a solution.

A Bright Idea

Evans Wadongo was born in a village in Kenya. His parents were both teachers, and they believed education was very important. They encouraged their children to work hard. Wadongo walked over six miles (9.6 kilometers) to elementary school every day. After school, he did his homework. However, as in many homes in rural Kenya, his house did not have electricity. So, at night, Wadongo had to do his homework by the light of a kerosene[1] lamp. 1

Wadongo began to have problems with his eyes. They hurt and this made studying difficult. He felt frustrated because his grades were not as good as he wanted. He realized that students who had electricity had an unfair advantage. "I couldn't compete with other kids who had access[2] 2

---

[1] *kerosene:* a type of oil that people use to provide heat and light

[2] *access:* opportunity to use something

"*I couldn't compete with other kids who had access to lighting.*"
— Evans Wadongo

to lighting," he said. "In every home in the village, it was the same. Many children drop out of school for this reason . . . so they remain poor for the rest of their lives."

Even though studying was difficult, Wadongo was an excellent student. After high school, he went to a university. While he was studying engineering, he continued to worry about kerosene lamps. By this time, he realized that kerosene was not just bad for schoolchildren. It was bad for the entire family. First, breathing kerosene fumes[3] can result in illnesses such as coughs. Also, the light from a kerosene lamp is not very strong, so reading by the light of a kerosene lamp can hurt people's eyes. In addition, this type of fuel burns very easily, which can lead to fires. Lastly, kerosene is expensive, so families have less money for food and other basic needs. It was difficult to come up with a different kind of lamp. Yet Wadongo did not give up. 3

He knew that a new lamp had to be inexpensive. He also believed the lamp should be good for the environment. One day he had an idea. He could use a very small solar light. Sunlight is free, and solar power is good for the environment. People could use this light instead of kerosene lamps. 4

Wadongo built his first solar lamp, and it worked. With the help of his friends and family, he began to build more lamps. He took these to local families who used kerosene lamps. An organization heard about his work. They decided to provide money for him to build more solar lamps. 5

Each lamp only cost $20 to build. However, this is a lot of money to many villagers, who only earn around $34 a week. So Wadongo made sure he kept the cost down. First, he used recycled 6

---

[3] *fumes:* unhealthy smoke and gases produced by burning

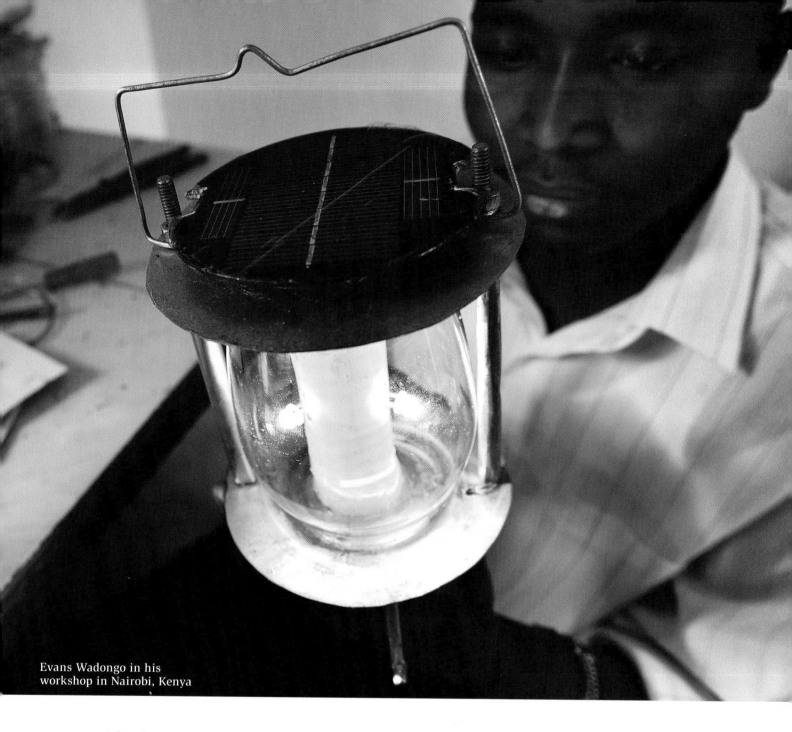

Evans Wadongo in his
workshop in Nairobi, Kenya

materials. This means he did not need to buy new materials. Next, volunteers built the lamps, so he did not have to pay salaries. Finally, people from many countries donated money to his organization. Therefore, the lamps were usually free.

Wadongo estimates he has delivered over 10,000 lamps. This means that thousands of people now have safe light. They do not have to use kerosene. Children can study at night, and because of this, they can stay in school. Families now have more money for food. As Julia Dzame, a mother of three children, says, "I am so grateful for the lights. My children will have light to read, and I'll have my own light to cook in the kitchen." Wadongo continues to work with his organization and he takes no salary. His reward[4] is his work. He knows that the lamps are not a long-term solution. He knows that all people should have electricity in their homes. Yet his solar lamps are helping people right now. "I want to reach out to as many rural communities as possible," he says. "The impact is saving lives."

7

---

[4] *reward:* something positive you get for doing a task well

READING COMPREHENSION

Big Picture

A The following statements are the main ideas of each paragraph in Reading 1. Write the correct paragraph number next to its main idea.

_____ **1.** Wadongo realized that students without electricity did not do well in school.

_____ **2.** Wadongo's parents encouraged him to work hard in school.

_____ **3.** Wadongo began to build more solar lamps.

_____ **4.** Kerosene lamps cause serious problems.

_____ **5.** Solar lamps improve the lives of rural families.

_____ **6.** Wadongo developed a lamp that is good for the environment.

_____ **7.** Wadongo was able to keep the cost of the lamps down.

B Compare answers to Exercise A with a partner. Then discuss what you think the main idea of the whole reading is.

Close-Up

Choose the answer that best completes each of the following sentences.

1. Wadongo was unhappy at school because _____.
   a. he had to drop out before he could finish
   b. he knew he could get better grades
   c. he was not as intelligent as the other students
   d. he did not have a solar lamp

2. According to the reading, children sometimes leave school because they _____.
   a. do not like learning
   b. cannot pay for their school
   c. find it difficult to study without electricity
   d. do not have enough kerosene lamps

3. Solar lamps are good for the environment because _____.
   a. they are free
   b. they do not use kerosene
   c. people can see better with these lamps
   d. they only cost $20 to make

4. Wadongo was able to keep the cost down because _____.
   a. he was a student at a university
   b. he knew the lamps had to be inexpensive
   c. the people who built the lamps worked for free
   d. he paid an organization to help build the lamps

5. According to the reading, Wadongo thinks that _____.
   a. solar lamps are a long-term solution
   b. rural families will never have electricity
   c. these lamps are only a short-term solution
   d. solar lamps are a better solution than electricity because they are free

Reading Skill

Identifying Supporting Details

In Unit 2, you learned that writers use specific details to support the main idea of a paragraph. (See page 30.) Supporting details are usually facts (names, numbers), reasons, and examples. Writers often use signals to introduce supporting details:

first, next, also, in addition, finally, lastly

for example, for instance, such as, including

one reason, experts believe, research shows

To identify supporting details:

- look for the main idea and highlight it
- look for signals that introduce supporting details that explain this main idea
- check that the details are specific, not general information

Note: Not all sentences in a paragraph provide supporting details. Writers often give background information to help you understand the topic. This information is often in the beginning of the paragraph.

A Read the following paragraph. As you read, underline the main idea. Number the supporting details. Then answer the questions below.

¹In India, over 400 million people have no access to electricity. ²This is a serious problem for several reasons. ³First, without electricity, children cannot study easily. ⁴Without education, they cannot get good jobs. ⁵Next, without electricity, people can't use computers and do not have access to the Internet. ⁶As a result, they don't learn important technology skills. ⁷Finally, without electricity, people stay home in the evenings. ⁸They do not go out to places such as shops, restaurants, and movie theaters. ⁹This means businesses do not develop and grow.

1. Which sentence provides the main idea? _____
2. Which sentence provides background information to the main idea? _____
3. Which signal words does the writer use? _____
4. Write the supporting details:

_____

_____

_____

B Reread paragraphs 3 and 6 in Reading 1. Underline the main ideas. Circle any signals. Number the supporting details.

VOCABULARY PRACTICE

Academic Vocabulary

(A) Find the words in the box in Reading 1. Use the context and the words in parentheses to help you choose the correct word to complete each of the following sentences.

encouraged (Par. 1)	materials (Par. 6)	estimates (Par. 7)
rural (Par. 1)	volunteers (Par. 6)	impact (Par. 7)

1. The United Nations _____ (guesses) that about 25 percent of the world does not have access to electricity.

2. In Bihar, India, the majority of people who live in _____ (farming) areas have no electrical power in their homes.

3. Having no electricity can have a very serious _____ (effect) on families in Bihar.

4. To try to solve this problem, the Indian government _____ (supported) research companies to work in Bihar.

5. _____ (unpaid workers) from these companies try to find inexpensive ways to bring electricity to farming areas.

6. One company, Husk Power Systems, has found a way to turn waste _____ (something you need to make other things) from rice into electricity.

(B) Work with a partner and complete each sentence with a word from the box. The correct word often appears with the word in bold. Give reasons for your choices.

areas	experts	help	huge	parents	recycled

1. In many schools, **volunteers** _____ young children learn to read.

2. Energy _____ **estimate** that the cost of gas will rise to more than six dollars a gallon by the end of the year.

3. People who live in **rural** _____ often grow some or all of their own food.

4. _____ **encourage** their children to study hard at school.

5. Education can have a(n) _____ **impact** on a child's life.

6. Many companies now use _____ **materials** to make new products.

Multiword Vocabulary

(A) Find the words in the box in Reading 1. Use the context and the words in parentheses to help you choose the correct multiword vocabulary to complete the following paragraph.

elementary school (Par. 1)	basic needs (Par. 3)	instead of (Par. 4)
drop out of school (Par. 2)	give up (Par. 3)	kept the cost down (Par. 6)

The United Nations estimates that each year, around 10 million children

_____ (stop attending) at the age of 11 to 12 years old. They stop
                    1
going to school for several reasons. Often, even _____ (primary
                                                                    2
education) is expensive. Schools have _____ (made it less
                                                          3
expensive) by giving out free books, for example. Yet children still need to buy a school uniform,

paper, and pens. These supplies can cost too much money for families who are very poor. Another

reason children _____ (stop trying) studying is that their
                              4
families need them at home. Some families do not have enough money for

_____ (necessary items for survival) such as food and clothing.
                    5
They need their children to help earn money. So, _____ (as a
                                                                    6
different action than) going to school, children have to stay home and help their parents.

B Compare your answers to Exercise A with a partner.

Use the Vocabulary

Write answers to the following questions. Use the words in bold in your answers. Then
share your answers with a partner.

1. What is your earliest memory from **elementary school**? Do you remember your first day at this
   school? What happened?

2. Do many students **drop out of school** in your country? If so, why?

3. Think of a sport that you tried but **gave up**. Why did you give it up?

4. How can **parents encourage** their children to study a subject they dislike?

5. How much do you **estimate** that the average student spends per week? What does the average
   student spend money on?

6. Going to a university is expensive. How can a student **keep down the costs**?

7. Do you prefer to live in a city or a more **rural area**? Why?

8. Why is it a good thing to be a **volunteer**? Have you ever been a **volunteer**? What did you learn
   from this experience?

THINK AND DISCUSS

Work in a small group. Use the information in the reading and your own ideas to
discuss the following questions.

1. **Identify problems.** What challenge faces many rural children in Kenya?

2. **Connect ideas.** How does Wadongo keep the cost of his lamps down?

3. **Express an opinion.** What do you think will happen to Wadongo and his organization in
   the future?

Academic Vocabulary

alternative	innovative	significant
to design	to provide	transportation

Multiword Vocabulary

to address a problem	environmentally friendly
to become increasingly popular	to get around
to come at a cost	a world record

Reading Preview

A **Preview.** Read the three headings in Reading 2. Then discuss the following questions with a partner or in a small group.

1. What methods of transportation do we use to travel by land? Which methods do you use the most to travel around your city?

2. How do we travel by water? By air?

3. Transportation can cause problems for the environment. What are some of these problems?

4. How are designers trying to make cars and trucks better for the environment?

B **Topic vocabulary.** The following words appear in Reading 2. Look at the words and answer the questions with a partner.

batteries	fuel	noise
complain	inventors	pollution
damage	mechanics	recharging
engineers	motor	

1. Which words are related to how an engine works?

2. Which words are about people?

3. Which words relate to problems that people sometimes have?

C **Predict.** What do you think this reading will be about? Discuss each word in Exercise B and predict how it may relate to the reading.

We like to get places fast. We travel by car or by plane. But this causes pollution. So what's the answer? Read about some exciting solutions to this worldwide problem.

Clean
TRAVEL

Eolian 3, the Chilean entry in a solar-powered car race, moves through the Atacama Desert in Chile. The three-day event in 2012 drew 15 teams from four countries.

E ach one of us shares this planet with seven billion other individuals. And we 1
all need transportation. People and products need to move from city to city
and country to country. However, the majority of cars, motorcycles, boats, and
planes cause pollution. They are also noisy. This is a serious problem in many cities.
So inventors are coming up with innovative ideas to try to reduce the pollution and
noise. Their ideas are not yet perfect. However, all great ideas begin somewhere.

By Land

In many cities around the world, motorcycles 2
are becoming increasingly popular. Currently,
Vietnam has around 33 million motorcycles. China
has almost 120 million. Motorcycles are a faster
and cheaper way to get around a city than cars.
Yet the convenience of these motorcycles comes
at a cost. Air pollution is a growing problem. In
large cities, people often complain it is difficult to
breathe. They also complain about the noise.

To solve these problems, a U.S. company 3
designed an environmentally friendly motorcycle. It
uses electricity as fuel. As a result, there is no pollution. You can drive it for 40 miles (64 kilometers)
before recharging the battery. It is also quiet and
fast—60 miles (96 kilometers) per hour. This makes
it a good choice for getting around a city.

By Water

The Italian city of Venice is a city with only 4
a few roads. There are no cars in the city center.
Instead of cars, water taxis and buses carry
people along the city's canals. The engines of
these boats are simple and cheap. However, they
cause pollution, particularly to the water. This
causes damage to the city's buildings.

English mechanics Dick Strawbridge and 5
Jem Stans designed a solar-powered water taxi.
The solar panels charge three electric batteries.
These, in turn, provide power to the engine. The
water taxi can carry six passengers. It can run
for a day. In the future, solar taxis could be an
alternative to Venice's current taxis.

By Air

Designing an environmentally friendly airplane is a real challenge. Planes use an enormous amount of jet fuel. This means they cause significant air pollution, and they are very noisy. Some major airplane manufacturers have started to address the problems. They are using cleaner fuels, for example. However, Swiss engineers have gone one step further. They developed a solar airplane—the *Solar Impulse*. Solar panels cover its wings. These panels provide power to four electric motors and batteries. The batteries allow the plane to fly at night. This plane holds the world record for the longest solar-powered flight—958 miles (1,541 kilometers) from Arizona to Texas in the United States.

READING COMPREHENSION

Big Picture

A Choose the answer that best completes each of the following sentences.

1. The main idea of paragraph 2 is that _____.
   a. China and Vietnam have around 155 million motorcycles
   b. motorcycles are noisy and cause air pollution

2. The main idea of paragraph 3 is that _____.
   a. a new motorcycle is pollution-free
   b. a new electric motorcycle can reach 60 miles per hour

3. The main idea of paragraph 4 is that _____.
   a. Venice is an unusual city
   b. boats are causing pollution in Venice

4. The main idea of paragraph 5 is that _____.
   a. the solar-powered water taxi may be a good alternative to water taxis in use today
   b. the soar-powered water taxi can carry up to six people

5. The main idea of paragraph 6 is that _____.
   a. planes use an enormous amount of jet fuel
   b. the *Solar Impulse* is good for the environment because it uses solar power instead of jet fuel

B Compare answers to Exercise A with a partner. Then write a sentence expressing the main idea of the *whole* reading.

_____

Close-Up

A Decide which of the following statements are true or false according to the reading. Write *T* (True) or *F* (False) next to each one.

_____ **1.** Inventors are trying to solve the problem of dirty and noisy transportation.

_____ **2.** Motorcycles are not as popular today as they were in the past.

_____ **3.** You can drive the electric motorcycle for 60 miles before recharging the battery.

_____ **4.** Venice has no roads and no cars in the city.

_____ **5.** Solar panels provide enough power to run the water taxi for a day before recharging.

_____ **6.** Some planes today are more environmentally friendly than other planes.

_____ **7.** Solar panels provide power to three electric batteries on the *Solar Impulse*.

B Work with a partner or in a small group. Change the false sentences in Exercise A to make them true.

Reading Skill

Understanding Pronouns

Writers do not always repeat important nouns. Instead, they use pronouns such as *he*, *she*, *it*, and *they*. *He* and *she* refer to a person; *it* refers to a thing; *they* refers to more than one person or thing.

Steve Jobs started Apple. **He** wanted to design innovative computers. Apple designed the first iPhone in 2007, and **it** quickly became very popular. Then Apple designed the next iPhone. Millions of people wanted the new phone. **They** waited for hours in Apple stores all over the world.

Writers use the pronoun *this* to refer to a whole idea.

People use kerosene lamps for heating, cooking, and light. However, **this** can cause health problems.

It is important to understand which word a pronoun refers to when you read. If you are not sure about the pronoun, you should
- look back to the beginning of the sentence. What person(s), thing(s), or idea(s) is the writer talking about?
- look back to the previous sentence. What person(s), thing(s), or idea(s) is the writer talking about?

A Read the following sentences. Underline the pronouns. Circle the noun or the whole idea that each pronoun refers to.

1. All over the world, people use flour for cooking. For example, they use it to make bread.

2. The cost of flour is increasing in some countries. This means bread is becoming more expensive.

3. An Indonesian woman decided to make bread from potatoes, not corn. Potatoes are cheaper than corn. She made the bread in her home and began to sell it.

4. A few months later, she won $2,200 in a business competition. This helped her to increase her business.

5. The magazine *Business World* wrote about this woman. It said that she was a good businesswoman. This made her famous in Indonesia.

B Reread paragraphs 2–6 of Reading 2 on pages 56–57. Underline the pronouns. Circle the noun(s) or the idea(s) the pronouns refer to.

VOCABULARY PRACTICE

Academic Vocabulary

A Find the words in bold in Reading 2. Use the context and the sentences below to help you choose the correct definition.

1. **Transportation** (Par. 1) is an important part of a country's economy.
   a. pollution
   b. way of moving people and things around
   c. solar power

2. Last year, our city came up with an **innovative** (Par. 1) way of helping people travel around the city. Residents can use one of the city's 5,000 bicycles.
   a. faster
   b. cheaper
   c. new

3. In the early 1900s, Thomas Edison **designed** (Par. 3) many innovative products such as the record player and the long-lasting light bulb.
   a. planned and made
   b. sold
   c. painted

4. In the future, the sun and the wind will **provide** (Par. 5) more power to people's homes.
   a. bring
   b. not pollute
   c. cost

5. Watching movies on a laptop has become an **alternative** (Par. 5) to watching movies on television.
   a. a complicated way of doing something
   b. a different way of doing something
   c. an easy way of doing something

6. People near the airport complained about the **significant** (Par. 6) increase in noise, particularly at night.
   a. small
   b. large
   c. fast

B The box below contains academic words from Exercise A and words they often appear with. Complete each sentence with a phrase from the box.

air transportation	a good alternative	provide jobs
design a product	innovative ways	significant changes

1. When companies _____, they have to think about who will use it, how easily it works, and how much it will cost.

2. People who are worried about the environment believe that we need more _____ to solve the problems connected with oil-based energy.

3. Technology has led to _____ in education. For example, students now learn very advanced computer skills at an early age.

4. The cost of _____ is very closely connected to the cost of oil. When oil prices increase, the cost of tickets usually increases as well.

5. Residents hope that the new factory will _____ in the area. This would help the many people who are looking for work.

6. More electric cars are now available. These cars are _____ to traditional, gas-based cars.

Multiword Vocabulary

Find the multiword vocabulary in bold in Reading 2. Then use the context and the sentences below to choose the correct answers.

1. Cell phones **are becoming increasingly popular** (Par. 2) because they can connect to the Internet and can take photos and videos.
   a. are being used a lot
   b. are being used more and more

2. I love my city because it is easy **to get around** (Par. 2) by foot and by bus.
   a. travel
   b. learn to drive

3. More people today have a car than in the past. However, this **comes at a cost** (Par. 2) to the environment.
   a. helps
   b. causes problems

4. Because bicycles are **environmentally friendly**, (Par. 3) cities are encouraging more people to use this form of transportation.
   a. fun to ride
   b. good for the earth

5. Cities are beginning to **address the problems** (Par. 6) of pollution by using more solar-powered buses and trains.
   a. solve the challenges
   b. understand the problems

6. Who has the **world record** (Par. 6) for winning the most Olympic gold medals?
   a. the biggest number
   b. the average number

Use the Vocabulary

Write answers to the following questions. Use the words in bold in your answers. Then share your answers with a partner.

1. What kinds of cars are **becoming increasingly popular** right now? Why do you think people like this type of car?

2. How can an individual live in an **environmentally friendly** way? Make a list of the things you can do to live in this way.

3. How do you **get around** your community? Do you use public **transportation**? Why or why not?

4. Think about a country or a city you have visited. What are some of the **significant** differences between that country or city and the place where you grew up?

5. Pollution from cars and motorbikes is a problem in almost every country. What are some governments doing to **address this problem**?

6. The Internet **provides** a huge amount of information. What kind of information do you search for on a daily basis?

7. Solar power is called an **"alternative"** fuel because it's not coal and it's not made from petroleum. What other types of alternative fuels are there?

THINK AND DISCUSS

Work in a small group. Use the information in the reading and your own ideas to discuss the following questions.

1. **Analyze.** What challenges face engineers as they try to design better forms of transportation?

2. **Identify problems.** What are some of the disadvantages, or problems, of an electric motorcycle, solar water taxi, and the *Solar Impulse*?

3. **Express an opinion.** How will methods of transportation change in the future?

Vocabulary Review

A Complete the paragraphs with the vocabulary below that you have studied in the unit.

comes at a cost	experts estimate	keeps the cost down	instead of
dropped out of school	huge impact	innovative way	recycled materials

   United Nations _____ that in Africa and Asia the average woman has to
1
walk six kilometers every day for clean water. In Ethiopia, Aylito Binayo is one of these women. Each

day, she leaves her rural home and walks for hours to get to clean water. It is hard, tiring work, and

it _____. Carrying heavy water causes a lot of injuries and takes a lot of time.
2
   In South Africa, Piet Hendrikse watched many women and children fetching water. He saw the

_____ this had on their health. He knew that many girls even
3
_____ to fetch water for their parents. So he came up with
4
a simple idea. He designed the Q-Drum. This is a large, plastic drum with

a hole in the middle. A woman fills it with 50 liters of water. Then she

puts a rope through the hole. _____ carrying the
5
water, she pulls it.

   Q-Drums are becoming increasingly popular, and not just in

Africa. Hendrikse's company is helping people in other countries to

make these drums. He encourages them to use

_____. This _____ because
6   7
the company doesn't have to buy many new materials. The Q-Drum is

definitely a simple, but _____ to carry water.
8

The Q-drum

B Compare answers to Exercise A with a partner. Then discuss the following questions.

*What are some of the effects of having no access to safe, clean water? Do you agree that the
Q-Drum is an innovative idea?*

C Complete the following sentences in a way that shows that you understand the
meaning of the words in bold.

1. **Parents** should **encourage** their children to _____.

2. After a fire destroyed several apartments, **volunteers helped** the families find _____.

3. _____ all help us **get around** cities easily.

4. For two years, I tried to get a job in Paris, but then I **gave up** and _____.

D Work with a partner and write four sentences that include any four of the vocabulary
items below. You may use any verb tense and make nouns plural if you want.

air transportation	get rid of	provide jobs
become increasingly popular	a good alternative	world record
environmentally friendly		

Connect the Readings

A The readings in this unit describe some serious global problems. They discuss some of the results of these problems, and they talk about some solutions.

1. Use information from Readings 1 and 2 to complete the following chart.

Problem	Results	Solution
They don't have electricity at home.		They drop out of school.
Kerosene lamps burn easily.		Solar lamp
Kerosene is expensive.		
	It causes problems with eyes and illnesses.	Solar lamp
Rural Kenyan families do not have a lot of money.	They can't afford expensive solar lamps.	
		Inventors are coming up with ideas to reduce pollution.
Venice relies on boats.		
Planes use a lot of jet fuel.		
Motorcycles		

2. Work with a partner. Think about the following ideas. What problems might happen as a result of these ideas? The first one has been done for you.

Idea	Problem
Solar lamps	*Families do not have electricity for a phone or for cooking.*
Volunteers build the solar lamps	
Solar-powered water taxis	
Electric motorcycles	
Solar-powered planes	

B With a partner or in a small group, compare answers to Exercise A. Then discuss the following questions.

1. Readings 1 and 2 explore some serious problems. Which do you think is the most serious problem?

2. Which is the most creative solution?

C Discuss the following questions with a partner. Use your understanding of the readings and your own ideas.

1. Some car companies offer electric cars as a good alternative to gas cars. However, not very many people buy electric cars. Why?

2. Think of another global problem. Are people finding innovative solutions to this problem?

Two women dry red peppers on
the ground in Jodhpur, India.

Food

FOCUS

1. What food do you eat a lot of? Do you eat much meat? Why? Why not?

2. Where does the food you eat come from? How much comes from local farmers?

Academic Vocabulary

| consumption | an income | to require |
| evidence | a portion | to tend to |

Multiword Vocabulary

a developing country	to put pressure on
in great demand	to take something for granted
natural resources	twice as much

Reading Preview

A Preview. Read the first sentence of each paragraph on pages 68–69. Then discuss the following questions with a partner or in a small group.

1. What do you usually have for breakfast? For lunch? For dinner?

2. What do you think is the connection between world population and the title of this reading?

3. Do you think it is a good idea to eat less meat? Why?

B Topic vocabulary. The following words appear in Reading 1. Look at the words and answer the questions with a partner.

billion	percent	shortage
corn	population	tripled
doubled	scarcer	wheat
hungry		

1. Which words relate to numbers?

2. Which words are names for different kinds of food?

3. A *crisis* is a very serious situation or problem. Which words relate to this word?

C Predict. What do you think this reading will be about? Discuss each word in Exercise B and predict how it may relate to the reading.

Every night, some people go to bed hungry. Can we solve this problem by changing what we eat? Find out why one expert thinks we can.

Eat Less Meat

A woman hangs up dry tofu in Iwadeyamacho, Japan.

1   Most of us grab breakfast as we leave home in the morning. Later, a quick hamburger makes a good lunch. At the end of the day, we sit down with our family or friends and enjoy dinner together. We take food for granted. We don't think about it. Yet experts argue a global food crisis is coming. This crisis is going to make us change the way we think about food.

2   Food prices are clear evidence of this crisis. Between 2005 and 2008, the cost of grains such as wheat and corn tripled. The price of rice was five times higher. In 2012, grain prices rose again by almost 50 percent. These rising prices show that food consumption is increasing more quickly than food production.

> *"The average American eats three hamburgers a week. That means Americans eat over 48 billion hamburgers every year."*

3   Food is in great demand because of a growing world population. Population grew slowly until 1800. Then it began to increase more quickly. By 1960, the population was three billion. It doubled to six billion by 1999 (see Figure 1). By 2050, this planet will need to feed at least nine billion people.

4   So, what can a hungry, crowded world do? One suggestion is to eat less meat. Meat uses more natural resources than grains. It requires more land to produce one pound (0.4 kilos) of meat than to produce one pound of grain. We use about one-third of the Earth's land to raise animals. It also requires between five and ten times more water than vegetable-based food. This is particularly serious

because of the global water shortage. Therefore, eating less meat will provide more land for farming, and it will save water.

To eat less meat, people will need ₅ to change their eating habits. That will not be easy. Americans, for example, have always loved meat. On average, they eat twice as much meat as people in other countries. They especially love hamburgers. The average American eats three hamburgers a week. That means Americans eat over 48 billion hamburgers every year. At the same time, as incomes rise in countries such as China and Brazil, the people in these countries tend to eat more meat. In developing countries, sales of meat have doubled in the last 20 years. They will double again by 2050. Growing global demand for meat will continue to put pressure on natural resources.

World population is increasing, resources ₆ are becoming scarcer, and food prices are rising. Therefore, we need to rethink our daily diet. For meat lovers, however, there is some good news. We don't need to give up meat entirely. "The solution isn't that everyone needs to become a vegetarian. Simply reducing portion[1] sizes . . . would go a long way," explains Eric Davidson. His solution: Eat more grains and less meat. Like many scientists worldwide, Davidson believes this is the only way to feed the nine billion mouths in 2050.

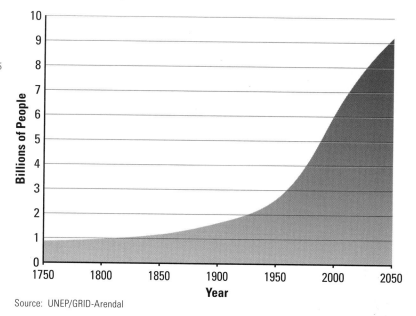

Figure 1: World Population Growth

Source: UNEP/GRID-Arendal

---

[1] *portion:* the amount of food served to one person at a meal

Dr. Mark Post

THE WORLD'S MOST EXPENSIVE BURGER

How long does it take you to buy a burger from a fast food restaurant? Perhaps five minutes? And how much does it usually cost? About five dollars? Burgers are fast, cheap, and tasty. Now imagine a burger that took two years to prepare and cost $325,000. But this was not an ordinary burger. It was created in a laboratory by a Dutch scientist, Dr. Mark Post. It uses a special type of meat that can grow in a laboratory. Dr. Post thinks this is the future of food. It requires less water, less land, and less energy. So it is more environmentally friendly than traditional meat. However, Dr. Post knows that there is a lot more research to do. Obviously, reducing costs is a major challenge. Then there is the question of the taste. The three lucky people who ate the world's most expensive burger said that it was dry. They also said that it did not taste very good!

READING COMPREHENSION

Big Picture

A The following statements are the main ideas of each paragraph in Reading 1. Write the correct paragraph number next to its main idea.

_____ **1.** The cost of food has increased in the last decade.

_____ **2.** We need to think more carefully about what we eat.

_____ **3.** If we eat less meat and more grains, we will be able to feed the world.

_____ **4.** People in many countries are eating more and more meat.

_____ **5.** Producing less meat is better for the environment.

_____ **6.** We need more food because of the rapidly growing population.

B Read the following statements. Check (✓) the statement that best expresses the main idea of the *whole* reading.

_____ **1.** There are several reasons why we should eat more grains.

_____ **2.** People need to eat less meat in order to have enough food for the future.

_____ **3.** The world's population is growing more quickly today than in the past.

_____ **4.** Food is getting more expensive because we eat too much meat.

_____ **5.** Scientists have found a new way to produce a more environmentally friendly meat.

Close-Up

Choose the answer that best completes each of the following sentences.

1. From 2005 to 2008, the price of wheat and corn _____.
  a. was higher than prices in 2012
  b. was lower than the previous decade
  c. rose by 50 percent
  d. increased a lot

2. According to paragraph 3 and Figure 1, in 2050 the world's population will be _____.
  a. fewer than 6 billion
  b. between 6 and 7 billion
  c. between 7 and 9 billion
  d. between 9 and 11 billion

3. According to paragraph 4, if people eat less meat, _____.
  a. food prices will fall
  b. farmers will use less water
  c. they will eat more grains and, therefore, will be healthier
  d. farmers will have less land to grow crops such as rice, corn, and wheat

4. Paragraph 5 states that when people earn more money, they often _____.
  a. eat less meat
  b. consume bigger portions of food
  c. eat more grains such as corn and less meat
  d. increase their meat consumption

5. According to paragraph 5, Davidson believes that people should _____.
   a. stop eating meat and become vegetarians
   b. not change their diets
   c. not eat as much meat as they do today
   d. decide for themselves what they eat

6. According the the short extra reading, "The World's Most Expensive Burger," on page 69, Dr. Post believes his burger is better for the environment than traditional meat because _____.
   a. it has taken scientists years to develop
   b. it uses fewer natural resources
   c. scientists developed it in a laboratory
   d. it tastes much better

Reading Skill

Understanding Graphs

When writers talk about numbers, they often focus on how numbers change. In Reading 1, for example, the writer talks about how the cost of food is increasing. Writers often include graphs to show how numbers are changing. Good readers pay attention to the graphs. They try to connect the numbers in the graph with the information in the reading.

In order to understand and talk about information in a graph, you should
- read the title carefully
- make sure you understand the two axes—the vertical (up and down) and horizontal (across) lines
- use the following verbs to talk about the numbers

Growing Numbers	Falling Numbers	No Change
rise (sharply, quickly, slowly)	fall (sharply, quickly, slowly)	stay the same
grow	decline	remain the same
increase	go down	
go up	be three times lower	
double		
triple		
be five times higher		

A Work with a partner to answer the following questions.

1. Reread paragraphs 2 and 3. Which words and phrases refer to changing numbers?

_____

2. Look at the graph in Figure 1 on page 69. What information is on the vertical axis?

_____

3. What information is on the horizontal axis? _____

4. What happened to world population between 1750 and 1850? _____

5. How did world population change between 1950 and 2000? _____

B Look at the graph below carefully. Then read the paragraph following it. Choose the correct words and phrases from the box to complete the paragraph. In some cases, more than one answer is possible.

| fall | increase | rose slowly | tripled | went up |

Figure 2: U.S. Corn Prices

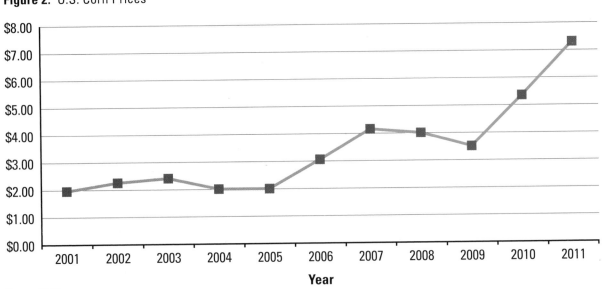

Source: USDA

Corn is in many things we use every day. Corn is in foods such as bread, sugar, and even chewing gum. It is in plastics and paper. It is in soap. It is in gas. So when the price of corn goes up, the cost of many other products may

_____ 1 , too. As Figure 2 shows, this happened from 2001 to 2011. The price of corn _____ 2 from 2001 to 2003. Then, after 2005, the cost suddenly _____ 3 . However, in 2007, the price started to

_____ 4 . Two years later, it once again increased until it was over seven dollars. In fact, between 2001 and 2011, the cost of corn more than _____ 5 . This means people are paying more for bread as well as many other items.

VOCABULARY PRACTICE

Academic Vocabulary

A Find the words in the box in Reading 1. Use the context and the words in parentheses below to help you complete the following sentences.

evidence (Par. 2)	requires (Par. 4)	tend to (Par. 5)
consumption (Par. 2)	incomes (Par. 5)	portion (Par. 6)

1. People who have a college degree usually have higher _____ (salaries) than people who do not have a degree.

2. Today, restaurants often serve larger _____ (amounts of food) sizes than they used to in the past.

3. A young child _____ (needs) fresh, nutritional food in order to be healthy and to grow properly.

4. Families who live in rural areas _____ (often) have better access to fresh food than people who live in the city.

5. _____ (facts and information) shows that right now, more people in the world live in cities than in rural areas.

6. Many experts believe that we need to increase our _____ (the amount we eat) of fruit and vegetables in order to be healthy.

B The words in bold often appear with the words on the right. Find the words in bold in Reading 1. Circle the word or words that appear with them in the reading.

1. _____ **evidence** (Par. 2)   clear / weak

2. _____ **consumption** (Par. 2)   gas / food

3. **requires** _____ (Par. 4)   less / between

4. **incomes** _____ (Par. 5)   are rising / are staying the same

5. **tend to** _____ (Par. 5)   eat / move

6. _____ **portion** sizes (Par. 6)   reducing / increasing

C Choose a word or phrase from the right column in Exercise B to complete each of the following sentences.

1. People are unhappy because **incomes** _____, but the cost of food, gas, and housing is increasing.

2. The police let the man go home because there was only _____ **evidence** connecting him with the crime.

3. My math teacher **requires** _____ homework than other teachers, but we have to go to the computer lab every day after class.

4. Parents **tend to** _____ closer to the city when their children have grown up and left home.

5. The study found that _____ **portion** sizes has led to a growing number of health problems, especially among children.

6. The city of Los Angeles is saving money on _____ **consumption** because its buses are now electric.

Multiword Vocabulary

Ⓐ Find the words in bold in Reading 1. Then use the words from the box below to complete the multiword vocabulary.

countries	demand	granted	much	on	resources

1. take (something) **for** _____ (Par. 1)

2. in great _____ (Par. 3)

3. natural _____ (Par. 4)

4. twice as _____ (Par. 5)

5. developing _____ (Par. 5)

6. put pressure _____ (Par. 5)

Ⓑ Complete the following sentences using the correct multiword vocabulary from Exercise A. Use the information in parentheses to help you.

1. A growing number of people in _____ (nations that do not have a lot of industry) now have access to the Internet.

2. In Korea, *kimchi* is _____ (very popular), but many Europeans think this food is too hot and spicy.

3. We need to take care of our _____ (things found in nature that humans use) such as water and forests because we cannot survive without them.

4. In China, rising incomes means more people can afford cars. This is beginning to _____ (have an impact) the demand for gas, and, as a result, gas prices are beginning to rise.

5. Gas in France costs _____ (double) as it costs in the United States.

6. Most people _____ clean water _____ (don't think about it). However, this might change if the water shortage gets more serious.

Use the Vocabulary

Write answers to the following questions. Use the words in bold in your answers. Then share your answers with a partner.

1. Name several **developing countries** around the world.

2. What are some of the **natural resources** of the country where you were born? Which natural resources are the most valuable?

The world's largest hamburger weighs in at 590 pounds (278 kilograms) in Toronto, Canada in May 2010.

3. Most parents **put pressure** on their children to act in certain ways. How do parents put pressure on teenagers?.

4. Some people think that gas will cost **twice as much** in the future. Do you agree? Explain your answer.

5. Many fast food restaurants offer "supersize" **portions**. Is it a good idea to eat such large amounts of food?

6. Some college teachers **require between** two and three hours of homework every night. Is this a reasonable amount of homework, or is it too much? Explain your answer.

THINK AND DISCUSS

Work in a small group. Use the information in the reading and your own ideas to discuss the following questions.

1. **Express an opinion.** Do you agree that people tend to take food for granted? What other resources do we take for granted?

2. **Analyze problems and identify solutions.** What are some of the problems with eating meat, according to the reading? What solutions does the reading offer?

3. **Apply knowledge.** Think of a country you know well. Do most people eat the same food as their grandparents did, or has their diet changed? If it has changed, is this a good or a bad thing?

Academic Vocabulary

available	creative	economic
a benefit	definitely	logical

Multiword Vocabulary

to be better off	a lack of
to catch on	to make sure that
inner-city	a practical solution

Reading Preview

A **Preview.** Read the title of Reading 2, look at the photos, and read the captions on pages 76–79. Then discuss the following questions with a partner or in a small group.

1. What does each photo have in common?

2. Why do you think someone is growing vegetables in the back of a truck?

3. Have you ever seen a building or truck like those in the photos? If so, where?

B **Topic vocabulary.** The following words appear in Reading 2. Look at the words and answer the questions with a partner.

fresh	local	organic
healthy	neighborhood	spinach
herbs	nutritional	urban
lettuce		

1. Which words are names of food?

2. Which words are about places?

3. Which adjectives describe food that is good for you?

C **Predict.** What do you think this reading will be about? Discuss each word in Exercise B and predict how it may relate to the reading.

What if you don't have a garden, but you want to grow your own food? Meet someone who has found an unusual way to solve this problem.

A "green" roof on top of Chicago's City Hall, in Chicago, Illinois, USA

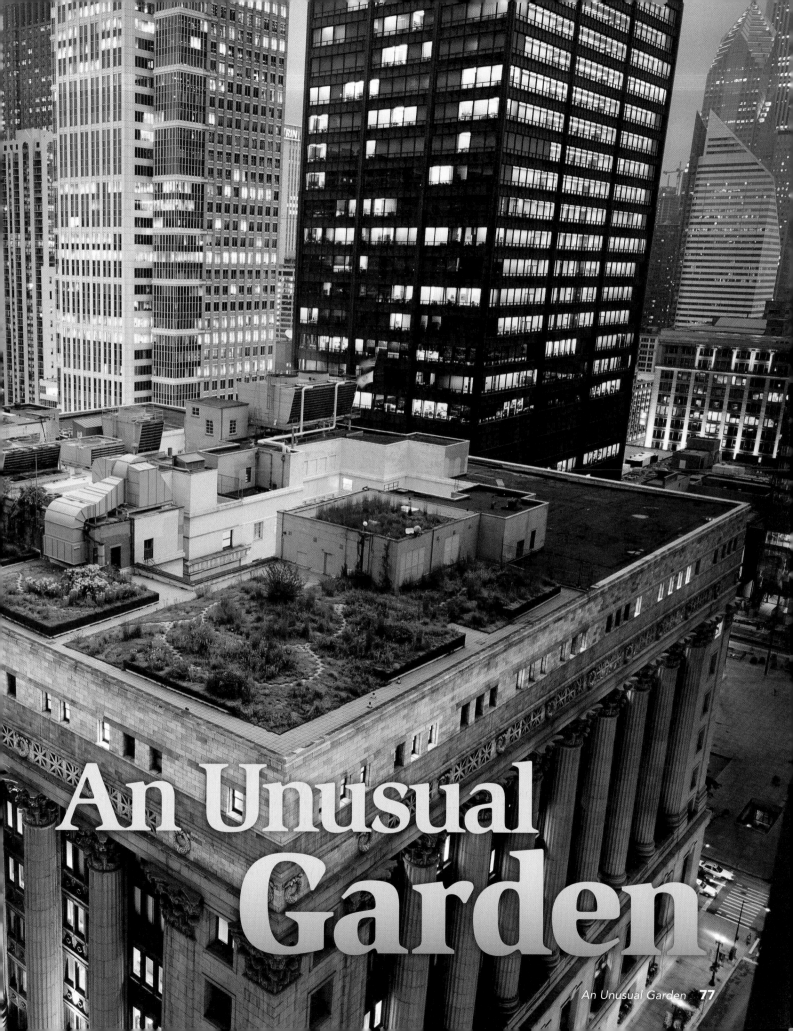

An Unusual Garden

The old 1986 truck was a gift from his grandfather. It worked, but it used a lot of gas. It was not an ideal vehicle for Ian Cheney's crowded, inner-city neighborhood in New York. Many New Yorkers would look at the truck and think of a junkyard.[1] Ian Cheney looked at his grandfather's truck and thought of a farm.

As in other large cities, there is not much space to grow food in New York. Yet Cheney wanted a vegetable garden. Many urban farmers in New York have found creative ways to grow vegetables. There are rooftop gardens high above the city. There are community gardens in old parking lots. There is even a floating garden in the Hudson River. Cheney, however, didn't have access to any of these spaces. So the old truck was a practical solution. The back of the truck provided him with the space he needed. "I don't have a rooftop to grow any food," Cheney explains. "It seemed like the logical thing to do."

So Cheney set to work. First, he drilled holes in the truck bed for drainage—allowing water to pass through the bed. Then he laid down a recycled plastic mat. The soil came next—a special lightweight variety. He made sure that everything was organic. Cheney preferred organic because he wanted to grow vegetables without chemicals. Then he planted lettuce, herbs, spinach, and tomatoes. Finally, he watered and waited.

When the food was ready to pick, Cheney drove the truck from one urban neighborhood to another. He gave away some of the vegetables. He sold the rest to friends and neighbors. Everywhere he parked, passersby stopped and talked about the beautiful vegetable garden in the back of the truck.

---

[1] *junkyard:* a place where you can buy parts of old cars

Vegetables grow in Ian Cheney's 1986 truck, parked on a New York city street.

Cheney is passionate about food. He strongly believes that people are better off eating more local food—that is, food grown close to where they live. Local food has both environmental and health advantages. It reduces "food miles." The term *food miles* refers to the distance between where you produce food and where you sell it. A lot of the food in large supermarkets travels hundreds of miles to get to your dinner table. This has an economic and environmental cost. Then there is the question of nutrition—food that helps you grow and be healthy. The nutritional benefits of vegetables decrease over time. So eating food within a few days of harvesting is healthier for you.

Cheney knows that his truck farm cannot solve the problem of the lack of fresh food in some neighborhoods. Yet, like rooftop gardens, it could be part of the solution. Cheney continues to plant his farm and drive it around New York neighborhoods. And the idea of local food is catching on. As Figure 1 shows, an increasing number of farmers' markets are selling local food in the United States. So fresh, local, and healthy food is now available in many places, including inner-city areas. As Cheney says, "If we can grow food in the back of an '86 Dodge pickup, we can definitely find better ways to grow more fresh produce."

Figure 1: Number of U.S. Farmers' Markets 1994–2012

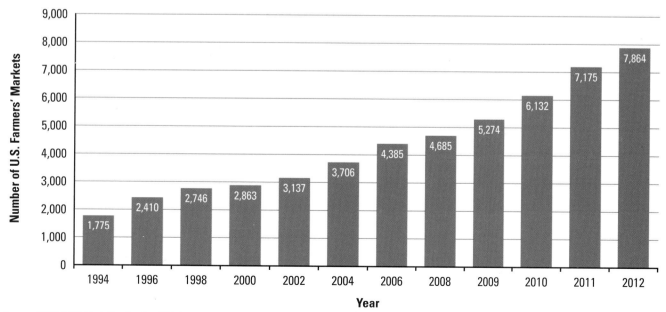

Source: USDA-AMS-Marketing Services Division

READING COMPREHENSION

Big Picture

Choose the answer that best completes each of the following sentences.

1. The main idea of the whole reading is that _____.
   a. a truck farm is a creative way to produce fresh, local food
   b. Ian Cheney grows vegetables in a truck
   c. New Yorkers have found creative ways to plant gardens

2. The main idea of paragraph 2 is that _____.
   a. Cheney did not have a rooftop for planting a garden
   b. city residents are finding creative ways to grow food
   c. Cheney thought of an unusual place to grow food in New York

3. The main idea of paragraph 3 is that _____.
   a. drainage is an important part of growing vegetables successfully
   b. there were several steps to building Cheney's truck farm
   c. Cheney planted organic vegetables because he prefers natural food

4. The main idea of paragraph 4 is that _____.
   a. Cheney enjoys talking to people
   b. neighbors wanted to know what Cheney was growing in his truck
   c. Cheney began to sell or give away his vegetables

5. The main idea of paragraph 5 is that _____.
   a. local food is better for people and the environment
   b. fresh and local vegetables taste better than store-bought vegetables
   c. some food travels a long distance to the grocery store

6. The main idea of paragraph 6 is that _____.
   a. the number of farmers' markets is increasing in the United States
   b. Cheney's truck farm is just part of the answer to growing more local food
   c. more New Yorkers are growing fresh food because of Ian Cheney

Close-Up

Ⓐ Decide which of the following statements are true or false according to the reading and Figure 1. Write *T* (True) or *F* (False) next to each one.

_____ 1. Cheney's truck uses a lot of gas, and this is expensive.

_____ 2. Cheney decided that growing vegetables in his truck was an easier choice for him than growing vegetables in his rooftop garden.

_____ 3. Cheney was worried that his truck bed wasn't big enough to grow vegetables.

_____ 4. Cheney sold his vegetables to local grocery stores.

_____ 5. Fresh food in supermarkets may come from many miles away.

_____ 6. Vegetables that take a long time to get to the supermarket have fewer nutritional benefits than local vegetables.

_____ 7. The number of farmers' markets in the United States more than doubled between 2000 and 2012.

_____ 8. From 2010 to 2012, the number of farmers' markets worldwide increased to 7,864.

B Work with a partner or in a small group. Change the false sentences in Exercise A to make them true.

Reading Skill

> ### Finding Definitions
>
> Sometimes readers are not sure about the meaning of a word or a phrase. However, if the word is important, writers often help you to understand the meaning. Writers do this in the following ways:
>
> - They use signals such as *or* and *that is* to explain the word.
>   **Life expectancy**—*that is, how long people live for*—*is increasing in all countries.*
>
> - They may use dashes, parentheses, or commas immediately after the word.
>   **Demography**, *the study of population, is an important subject in today's world.*
>
> - They use examples to explain the meaning.
>   **Dairy products** *such as milk, cheese, and yogurt are an important part of your daily diet.*

A Read the following paragraph. Look for definitions or examples that explain important words. Circle these words. Underline the definitions.

Too many Americans are eating too much salt, a report has recently stated. Doctors say that most young, healthy adults should have about 2,300 milligrams of salt per day. However, most Americans are consuming more than 3,400 milligrams with their daily meals. Your body needs some salt. However, if you have too much, it accumulates, or builds up, in your blood. This can lead to serious health problems such as a stroke, a serious illness in our brain. To reduce salt in your diet, you can read food labels to determine, that is to figure out, the amount of salt in that food. You should avoid processed food such as chips and frozen dinners. The best advice? Eat plenty of fresh, local fruit and vegetables.

B Look back at Reading 2. Find definitions of the following words and fill in the chart.

Words	Definitions
1. drainage (Par. 3)	
2. organic (Par. 3)	
3. local food (Par. 5)	
4. food miles (Par. 5)	
5. nutrition (Par. 5)	

VOCABULARY PRACTICE

Academic Vocabulary

Ⓐ Find the words in bold in Reading 2. Use the context and the sentences below to help you match each word to the correct definition.

_____ **1.** City residents often think of very **creative** (Par. 2) ways to grow food.

_____ **2.** Moving to a city is a **logical** (Par. 2) decision for many people. There are more jobs in the city.

_____ **3.** Although many people still do not have a job, the **economic** (Par. 5) situation is slowly improving.

_____ **4.** There are many health **benefits** (Par. 5) to growing your own food. For example, it is fresher and you get exercise while you work in your garden.

_____ **5.** The computers in the library are now **available** (Par. 6) 24 hours a day.

_____ **6.** Fruit is **definitely** (Par. 6) a healthier snack than candy.

a. certainly; without doubt

b. imaginative and new

c. advantages; things that help you

d. sensible; reasonable

e. connected to business and industry

f. able to be used

Ⓑ Choose the correct word from the box to complete each of the following sentences. Notice and learn the words in bold because they often appear with the academic words.

available	benefits	creative	economic	logical

1. Steve Jobs was well-known for his _____ **ideas** in the world of technology.

2. The country faces several _____ **problems** such as the rising cost of food and the growing number of people without work.

3. James decided to leave his job and travel around Asia. It wasn't a(n) _____ **thing to do**, but he wanted to travel while he was still young.

4. The company announced that the new phone is **now** _____ in stores.

5. The **health** _____ of eating more fish and less meat are clear, according to my doctor.

Multiword Vocabulary

Ⓐ Find the multiword vocabulary in bold in Reading 2. Use the context to help you understand the meaning. Then match each item to the correct definition.

_____ **1. inner-city** (Par. 1)

_____ **2. a practical solution** (Par. 2)

_____ **3. made sure that** (Par. 3)

_____ **4. are better off** (Par. 5)

_____ **5. the lack of** (Par. 6)

_____ **6. is catching on** (Par. 6)

a. not enough

b. a sensible answer to a problem

c. are more successful

d. is becoming more popular

e. relating to the area near the center of a large city

f. checked that something is the way you want it

B Complete the following sentences with the correct multiword vocabulary from Exercise A.

1. Electric cars _____. More people are buying them today even though they are still quite expensive.

2. The teacher _____ the students were ready for the test.

3. Parents are complaining about _____ space where children can play. They are trying to get the government to create more parks.

4. _____ apartments are very expensive, so many people live outside the city and drive long distances to work.

5. The two students could not afford to rent their own apartment, so they came up with _____. They found a third friend and rented an apartment together.

6. Most experts agree that people with university degrees _____ than people with only high school diplomas.

Use the Vocabulary

Write answers to the following questions. Use the words in bold in your sentences. Then share your answers with a partner.

1. Some students choose to live in student housing. Other students prefer to rent their own apartments. What are some of the **benefits** of each of these two choices? Which would you prefer to live in—an apartment or student housing?

2. Do you think you will **be better off** than your grandparents? Your parents? Explain your answer.

3. If high school students in your country want to go to a university, do they have a lot of choices **available** to them? What are some of these choices?

4. "It is **definitely** an advantage to be able to speak English in today's global world." Do you agree with this statement? What other languages are important to learn?

5. Teachers should **make sure that** their students understand what they are learning. How did your high school teachers make sure you understood everything?

6. Would you prefer to live in an **inner-city** area or in a rural area? Explain your answer.

THINK AND DISCUSS

Work in a small group. Use the information in the reading and your own ideas to discuss the following questions.

1. **Identify problems and find solutions.** Why is it a challenge to grow vegetables in New York City? What are residents doing to solve this problem?

2. **Summarize.** Why is local food better for you, according to the reading?

3. **Analyze.** Define the term *food miles*. Why is there an *environmental cost* to food miles?

Vocabulary Review

A Complete the paragraphs with the vocabulary below that you have studied in the unit.

are catching on	lack of
creative ideas	logical thing to do
health benefits	take it for granted
in great demand	twice as much

Will Allen

Did you know that the average Swedish breakfast travels 24,901 miles from farm to table? Two reasons explain why food is traveling farther today. First, we _____ that we can eat
1
any fruit or vegetables whenever we want. And fresh fruit is _____.
2
People in England want strawberries in winter, for example. So stores fly this fruit from warm countries such as Chile. The second reason is money. Costs are lower in developing countries. For example, Norwegian fishermen send fish to China. There, factories prepare the fish and fly it back to Norway, where people buy it for dinner. This doesn't seem like a _____. Yet it costs more than
3
_____ to prepare the fish in Norway as it does in China.
4

Will Allen, a professional basketball-player turned farmer, is working hard to reduce food miles. When he started his farm, he saw that there was a _____ fresh food in
5
the urban area where he lived. Knowing the _____ of eating local, fresh food,
6
he started to sell vegetables to his neighbors. He also wanted to teach his neighbors how to grow their own food in the city. He has come up with some _____ such as growing
7
vegetables in water and turning parking lots into small farms. His ideas _____
8
as more people in his area are buying his food and learning how to grow their own.

B Compare answers to Exercise A with a partner. Then discuss the following questions.

Why does food travel longer distances today? Why does the writer suggest that it is not logical to send Norwegian fish to China?

C Complete the following sentences in a way that shows that you understand the meaning of the words in bold.

1. Today, people **tend to eat** more _____.

2. Although **incomes are rising** in some countries, in other countries _____.

3. Small cars **require less** _____.

4. In my city, there is a serious **lack of** _____.

D Work with a partner and write four sentences that include any four of the vocabulary items below. You may use any verb tense and make nouns plural if you want.

available now	definitely	inner city
be better off	economic problems	make sure that

Connect the Readings

A Writers use specific details to support general statements. Use information from Readings 1 and 2 to add specific details to the following statements. One answer has been done for you.

Important Idea	Specific Details
1. World population began to grow more quickly in the 20th century.	
2. Food prices have increased in the last decade.	
3. Experts predict that population will continue to grow in the 21st century.	
4. Growing grain is better for the environment than producing meat.	
5. The demand for meat in some developing countries is increasing.	
6. Urban farmers have found creative ways to grow their own food in small spaces.	*rooftop gardens, truck farm, floating gardens*
7. Ian Cheney used environmentally friendly ways to make his truck farm.	
8. In the last decade, Americans have been able to buy more local, fresh food.	

B With a partner or in a small group, compare answers to Exercise A. Then discuss the following questions.

1. What global problem does this unit discuss?

2. What solutions do Readings 1 and 2 offer to this problem?

C Discuss the following questions with a partner. Use your understanding of the readings and your own ideas.

1. What kinds of food do you eat regularly? Where does this food come from?

2. Is local food available where you live? Is organic food available?

Ida, a 47 million-year-old fossil, on view at the American Museum of Natural History in New York, New York, USA

Natural History

FOCUS

1. A fossil is an impression or part of something that lived millions of years ago. Look at the photo on this page. What type of animal, insect, or plant can you see?

2. What can fossils tell us about the past?

READING 1

Academic Vocabulary

to contain	enormous	therefore
dramatically	specific	typical

Multiword Vocabulary

compared to	freezing cold
to fast-forward	a long time ago
to figure out	to make a discovery

Reading Preview

A Preview. Read paragraph 1 on page 90. Look at the photos. Then discuss the following questions with a partner or in a small group.

1. In which photo can you see the area described in the first paragraph?

2. What are some of the differences in the two areas shown in the photo on pages 88 and 89?

3. Would you like to visit this area today? Why, or why not?

B Topic vocabulary. The following words appear in Reading 1. Look at the words and answer the questions with a partner.

chemicals	insects	plants
dinosaurs	nitrogen	stone
frozen	oxygen	wood
ice		

1. Which words are related to fossils?

2. Which words are most closely related to science?

3. Which words are about very cold temperatures?

C Predict. What do you think this reading will be about? Discuss each word in Exercise B and predict how it may relate to the reading.

What was the weather like yesterday? That's easy to answer. What was it like millions of years ago? Not so easy. Discover how scientists find out about the weather of the past.

Nature's Clues

It's a typical day on Axel Heiberg Island, an area in the Arctic near the North Pole.[1] The weather is beautiful and sunny—almost tropical. There are enormous trees and many plants. The warm air smells of flowers. Birds are singing. The forest is full of animals and insects. Alligators are lying quietly in the lakes.

That was 45 million years ago. Now fast-forward to today. The temperature is –10 degrees Celsius (14 degrees Fahrenheit). The wind makes it feel colder. Nothing moves. It is silent and freezing cold. The weather on the island is dramatically different now than it was in the past.

How do we know what the weather was like millions of years ago? One way scientists learn about ancient climates is by studying fossils.

---

[1] *North Pole:* an area in the Arctic Ocean that is the most northern point on Earth

Scientists find fossils of insects, dinosaurs, leaves, and even whole trees. They know that different living things survive in different climates. For

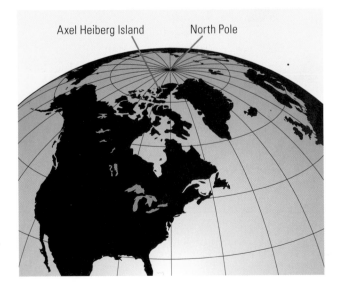

Axel Heiberg Island in Nunavut, Canada, where scientists have discovered large fossil forests

example, tropical plants need warm weather and lots of rain. Therefore, when scientists find fossils from tropical plants, they can begin to figure out what the weather was like millions of years ago in that area.

Scientist Hope Jahren made a very important 4 discovery on Axel Heiberg Island. In 2001, she discovered rare wood fossils on the island. She was surprised that trees once grew near the North Pole. How was that possible? Jahren found clues in the wood fossils. Unlike most fossils, these wood fossils never turned into stone. In fact, they look like old, dry wood. Most importantly, they still contain chemicals, including oxygen and nitrogen. These chemicals came from the soil, water, and air from a long time ago. They give specific information about rain and temperatures.

From the unusual wood fossils, Jahren 5 realized that today's frozen island was once very warm and wet. "The Earth today is very different compared to how it was millions of years ago," she explains. Jahren continues to study fossils because they can teach us about climate change in the past. This can help us understand and prepare for climate change today.

READING COMPREHENSION

Big Picture

(A) Choose the statement that best completes each of the following sentences.

1. Paragraph 1 describes _____.
   a. a tropical island
   b. Axel Heiberg Island today
   c. an area near the North Pole millions of years ago

2. The main idea of paragraph 2 is that _____.
   a. at certain times of the year, the temperature on the island is -10 degrees Celsius
   b. today's weather on the island is very different than it was in the past
   c. ice covers large areas of the Arctic including this island

3. The main idea of paragraph 3 is that _____.
   a. scientists learn about ancient climates by studying fossils
   b. scientists study fossils of plants, insects, and dinosaurs
   c. different plants require different temperatures and amounts of rainfall

4. The main idea of paragraph 4 is that _____.

   a. in 2001, Hope Jahren found some plant fossils near the North Pole

   b. millions of years ago, trees grew on Axel Heiberg Island

   c. wood fossils provide information about ancient climates

5. The main idea of paragraph 5 is that _____.

   a. studying fossils helps scientists to understand today's changing climate

   b. climate change is a serious problem for Axel Heiberg Island

   c. Jahren discovered that the weather on Axel Heiberg was much hotter in the past

B Compare answers to Exercise A with a partner. If you have different answers, go back to Reading 1 to find the correct answer.

Close-Up

A Choose the best answer for each of the following questions, according to the reading.

1. What is the weather usually like most days on Axel Heiberg Island?

   a. warm and sunny   **b.** very cold

2. What kind of information do we learn from fossils?

   a. how fossils turn into wood   **b.** what kinds of creatures and plants lived in the past

3. What did Jahren realize when she found the wood fossils?

   a. The fossils contained insects and leaves.   **b.** Trees once grew in this icy land.

4. Which sentence is NOT correct, according to the reading?

   a. The majority of fossils are made of stone.   **b.** Unlike stone fossils, wood fossils do not contain chemicals.

5. Read the following sentences. What does *they* refer to?

   *Jahren found clues in the wood fossils. Unlike most fossils, these wood fossils never turned into stone. In fact, **they** look like old, dry wood.*

   a. Jahren's clues   **b.** most fossils   **c.** wood fossils

6. Why was Jahren's discovery important?

   a. She found the fossils on an island.   **b.** The wood fossils contained certain chemicals.

7. Read the following sentences. What does *this* refer to?

   *Jahren continues to study fossils because they can teach us about climate change in the past. **This** can help us understand and prepare for climate change today.*

   a. Jahren continues to study fossils.   **b.** Fossils teach us about climate change in the past.

8. What is the purpose of Jahren's research?

   a. to understand climate change   **b.** to explain how living things survived in the past

B Compare answers to Exercise A with a partner. If you have different answers, go back to Reading 1 to find the correct answer.

Reading Skill

Scanning for Specific Information

We read for different purposes. Sometimes we need to understand the main idea of a reading. We usually read the whole text to find main ideas. Other times, however, we only need to find specific information—that is, a detail. Then we do not need to read everything. We can quickly look over the reading, or scan, for the specific information.

When you scan for information, you should

- decide what information you need (Is it a name, a place, a number?)
- find an important, or key, word to help find this information
- quickly look over the reading (Don't read it all; just look for the key word.)

When you find the key word, carefully read the information around the word to make sure you have found the correct information.

A Read the following questions. Focus on the key words in bold. Then quickly scan the paragraph below for the answers. Write short answers on the lines.

1. What is a **paleontologist**? _____

2. **When** did **dinosaurs** disappear? _____

3. What is an **asteroid**? _____

4. **Where** did the asteroid hit Earth? _____

5. How big was the **crater**? _____

    Paleontologists are scientists who study fossils. These experts want to know why dinosaurs disappeared from Earth about 65 million years ago. They believe an asteroid—that is, a rock that travels through space—was responsible. Around that time, a large asteroid smashed into Yucatán, an area in southeastern Mexico. It made a huge crater, or hole, in the ground. The crater was over a hundred miles wide. Paleontologists believe this asteroid changed the world's climate. They think that dust from the asteroid blocked the sunlight. Plants could not grow. As a result, dinosaurs and 70 percent of all other living things disappeared at this time.

B Read the following questions about Reading 1. Underline the key word(s) in each question. Then scan the reading to find the answers. Write short answers on the lines.

1. What is the temperature on Axel Heiberg Island today? _____

2. What kind of weather do tropical plants need? _____

3. What do fossils usually turn into? _____

4. When did Jahren discover the wood fossils? _____

5. Which chemicals did she find in the wood fossils? _____

VOCABULARY PRACTICE

Academic Vocabulary

(A) Find the words in bold in Reading 1. Use the context and the sentences below to match each bold word to the correct definition.

_____ 1. Learning how to get around the city is a **typical** (Par. 1) problem for visitors.

_____ 2. The Burj Khalifa building in Dubai is **enormous** (Par. 1)— 830 meters high.

_____ 3. The price of gas fell **dramatically** (Par. 2) last month.

_____ 4. It was snowing and very cold. **Therefore,** (Par. 3) we stayed inside.

_____ 5. Many websites **contain** (Par. 4) interesting information.

_____ 6. Please give me more **specific** (Par. 4) information.

a. as a result

b. sharply

c. normal

d. very big

e. have

f. detailed

(B) Read each of the following sentences. Choose the word or phrase that does _not_ usually appear with the word in bold. Then mark the wrong word with an X.

1. In a **typical** _____, I drink two cups of coffee.
   a. day   b. morning   c. decade

2. That is an **enormous** _____.
   a. problem   b. difference   c. answer

3. The price _____ **dramatically**.
   a. stayed the same   b. fell   c. increased

4. This is a **specific** _____.
   a. question   b. idea   c. Earth

5. The glass bottles **contain** _____.
   a. degrees   b. chemicals   c. milk

Multiword Vocabulary

(A) Find the multiword vocabulary in bold in Reading 1. Use the context to help you understand the meaning. Then match each item to the correct definition.

_____ 1. **fast-forward** (Par. 2)

_____ 2. **freezing cold** (Par. 2)

_____ 3. **figure out** (Par. 3)

_____ 4. **made a** very important **discovery** (Par. 4)

_____ 5. **a long time ago** (Par. 4)

_____ 6. **compared to** (Par. 5)

a. understand

b. when contrasted with

c. found or learned something new

d. move ahead to

e. below 32 degrees Fahrenheit

f. many years in the past

B Complete the following sentences with the correct multiword vocabulary from Exercise A.

1. Fish fossils show that water covered this dry land _____.

2. New technology allows you to very quickly _____ to the part of the movie you want to watch.

3. Average temperatures seem to be higher _____ 100 years ago.

4. The students couldn't _____ the answer to the math problem.

5. Animals such as polar bears can live in _____ temperatures.

6. Alexander Fleming _____ in the 1920s: He found a new type of medicine, which he called penicillin.

Use the Vocabulary

Write answers to the following questions. Use the words in bold in your answers. Then share your answers with a partner.

1. What do you do on a **typical** Saturday?

2. Our lives change a lot as we get older. Give some examples of how your life today is **dramatically** different than it was five years ago.

3. What is an **enormous problem** you have faced?

4. What kind of music do you enjoy? Give a **specific** example of a band or a singer.

5. Complete the following sentence: *I often don't understand when people speak English;* **therefore,** *I should . . .*

6. Think about your life today. Now **fast-forward** five years. How will your life be different?

7. Some people live in areas where it is **freezing cold** in the winter and very hot in the summer. Would you enjoy this kind of climate? What is your idea of a perfect climate?

THINK AND DISCUSS

Work in a small group. Use the information in the reading and your own ideas to discuss the following questions.

1. **Connect ideas.** How are the wood fossils from Axel Heiberg Island different from most fossils?

2. **Use what you know.** Reading 1 explains how fossils can provide information about past climates. What other information can fossils give us about life long ago?

3. **Express an opinion.** Hope Jahren is a scientist who studies fossils. Do you think this is an interesting career? Explain your answer.

Academic Vocabulary

to conserve	to depend	a series
current	a resident	to support

Multiword Vocabulary

as many as possible	on a regular basis
to be concerned	once more
during times of	on record

Reading Preview

A **Preview.** Look at the photos on pages 96–98. Read the captions, or words, below the photos. Then discuss the following questions with a partner or in a small group.

1. Why are the people climbing the tree in the photo?

2. How does climate change affect trees?

3. What can trees tell us about weather in the past?

B **Topic vocabulary.** The following words appear in Reading 2. Look at the words and answer the questions with a partner.

desert	findings	samples
drought	rainfall	scientist
examined	research	tested

1. Which word describes a place that has very little rain?

2. Which words are about a shortage of water?

3. Which words refer to studying new information?

C **Predict.** What do you think this reading will be about? Discuss each word in Exercise B and predict how it may relate to the reading.

A scientist can learn a lot from a tree. Find out how a simple piece of wood can tell us about the past and the present.

Scientists measure a giant sequoia tree in California, USA.

The Answer is in the Trees

THE ANSWER IS IN THE TREES

Dave Meko lives in Arizona, in the southwestern United States. Like other residents, he noticed that 1999 was a hot, dry year. The following year was also dry. So was 2001. The year after that was the driest on record. Water levels in the huge Colorado River were dropping rapidly. This was the beginning of a serious drought. Everyone began asking, "How long will it last?" Meko, a scientist at the University of Arizona, believed that he could find the answer in the trees. 1

Meko is a tree-ring expert. He studies the rings within a tree to find information about climate change. Each year, a tree adds a new layer of wood. These layers look like a series of rings. During times of heavy rainfall, a ring is wide. When there is a shortage of water, a ring is narrow. These rings are nature's record of rainfall and climate change. 2

Meko knew that people were right to be concerned about the low water in the Colorado River. This river supplies water to over 30 million people in seven states as well as parts of Mexico. Cities such as Las Vegas, Phoenix, and Los Angeles depend on it. Without the Colorado River, this land would once more become desert. 3

Fossilized tree in Arizona, USA, provides clues to rainfall from the past.

So Meko was not surprised when people began to worry, and his phone started ringing.

Meko and his team quickly started a new research project. Their goal was to find out how long previous droughts lasted. The team collected as many old wood samples as possible. They tested wood samples from 1,200 years ago until the present. When they examined the rings, the news about rainfall in the past was not good.

Meko's research showed that the 20th century was an unusually wet time. Trees from this period had wide, healthy rings. Rain was plentiful. During that century, millions of people moved to the region. Before that time, however, the rings showed that droughts occurred on a regular basis. In fact, drought was part of the usual climate pattern. There were severe droughts in the 900s, the 1100s, and the late 1200s.

"Each year, a tree adds a new layer of wood. These layers look like a series of rings."

Human history seems to support Meko's findings. The native Anasazi lived in this area for hundreds of years, starting around 500 AD. They were farmers and depended on water to grow their crops. However, at the end of the 13th century, the Anasazi suddenly left the area. Experts do not know exactly why the Anasazi left. They think it was because there was no longer enough water to farm. And Meko's tree rings clearly show a severe drought at that time.

How long will the current drought last? Using nature's clues from the past, experts predict that this drought may continue for another 50 years. This is a serious problem for residents in the area. They will probably not leave the area like the Anasazi, but they will need to conserve water during this long dry period.

READING COMPREHENSION

Big Picture

Ⓐ Choose the statement that best completes each of the following sentences.

1. The main idea of the whole reading is that _____ .
   a. tree rings explain why the Colorado River is low
   b. Dave Meko studies tree rings in order to learn about climate change
   c. Dave Meko is an expert in tree-ring research

2. The main idea of paragraph 2 is that _____ .
   a. tree rings give information about the climate
   b. a wide ring means that there was normal rainfall
   c. Meko studies tree rings

3. The main idea of paragraph 3 is that _____ .
   a. many people called Meko about the weather
   b. water levels in the Colorado River are dropping
   c. millions of people depend on the Colorado River

4. The main idea of paragraph 4 is that _____ .
   a. Meko's team started to find information about the 1200s
   b. the team quickly began their research
   c. Meko's team examined wood in order to find out about the past

B Answer the following questions in complete sentences.

1. What is the main idea of paragraph 5?

2. What is the main idea of paragraph 6?

3. What is the main idea of paragraph 7?

Close-Up

A Decide which of the following statements are true or false according to the reading. Write *T* (True) or *F* (False) next to each one.

_____ 1. Arizona had more rain in 2002 than the year before.

_____ 2. When rainfall is normal, a tree ring is wider than when there is a drought.

_____ 3. Falling water levels in the Colorado River is a serious problem for areas such as Las Vegas.

_____ 4. From 1900 to 1999, the weather was much wetter than in the centuries before this time.

_____ 5. Meko's tree-ring research shows that droughts in this area of the United States are very unusual.

_____ 6. The late 1200s experienced a period of very hot and wet weather.

_____ 7. Although scientists are not completely sure, they believe the Anasazi people had to leave the area because of a serious drought.

_____ 8. Research shows that the drought today will probably continue for another few decades.

_____ 9. Tree rings provide information about the weather from a long time ago, and this helps scientists understand today's climate.

B Work with a partner or in a small group. Change the false sentences in Exercise A to make them true.

Reading Skill

Organizing Information in Outlines

In previous units, you learned that a writer uses details to support the main idea of a paragraph. For this reason, it is a good idea to take notes on main ideas and supporting details. This helps academic readers understand the reading. It also makes it easier to remember important information.

An outline is one way to take notes. There are different ways to outline. However, a good outline clearly shows the main idea and the most important supporting details.

As you prepare to outline a paragraph, you should
- look for the main idea and highlight it
- look for supporting details and number them

A Find supporting details in the following paragraph to complete the outline.

The Colorado River is one of the United States' longest rivers. It is also one of the most important because it provides water to a large area that has little rain. Many farms depend on the river. Farmers use 66 percent of it to water their crops. In fact, the river provides water to more than 3.5 million acres of farmland. Cities also need the river. Cities such as Phoenix use the other 33 percent of the water.

Main Idea: A large area depends on the Colorado River.

A. Farms depend on it.

- _____

- _____

B. _____

- _____

- Phoenix is an example a city that depends on river.

B Reread paragraphs 2 and 3 from Reading 2 on pages 98–99. As you read, underline the main idea. Number the supporting details. Then use your underlining to complete the following outlines.

1. (Par. 2) Main Idea: Tree rings give information about climate change.

    A. Each year—_____

       - Series of rings

    B. Normal rainfall

       - _____

    C. _____

       - narrow ring

2. (Par. 3) Main Idea: Millions of people depend on the Colorado River.

    A. 30 million people

       - _____

    B. Cities

       - _____

    C. Without the river, _____

VOCABULARY PRACTICE

Academic Vocabulary

A Find the words in bold in Reading 2. Then use the context to help you match each word to its correct definition.

1. A **series** (Par. 2) is _____.
2. If you **depend** (Par. 3) on someone, _____.
3. If you **support** (Par. 6) something, _____.
4. When something is **current** (Par. 7), _____.
5. **Residents** (Par. 7) are _____.
6. When you **conserve** (Par. 7) something, _____.

a. it is happening right now
b. you make it stronger
c. you need that person
d. several things that come after each other
e. you prevent it from being wasted
f. people who live in a specific place

B Chose the correct word from the box to complete each of the following sentences. The words in bold can help you because they often appear with the academic words.

| conserve | current | depend | residents | series | support |

1. Many people in big cities _____ **on** public transportation to get around.
2. We can _____ **water** by taking shorter showers.
3. Scientists must _____ **research** with detailed information.
4. **Apartment** _____ heard the alarm and quickly left the building.
5. You can go online to find out about _____ **weather** conditions.
6. A _____ **of large storms** hit the city, one after the other.

Multiword Vocabulary

A Find the words in bold in Reading 2. Then use the words from the box below to complete the multiword vocabulary.

| about | during | on | once | possible | regular |

1. _____ **record** (Par. 1)
2. _____ **times of** (Par. 2)
3. **to be concerned** _____ (Par. 3)
4. _____ **again** (Par. 3)
5. **as many** (things/people) **as** _____ (Par. 4)
6. **on a** _____ **basis** (Par. 5)

Ⓑ Complete the following sentences with the correct multiword vocabulary from Exercise A. Use the information in parentheses to help you.

1. Evidence shows that people are correct _____ (to be worried) the Colorado River. It may not have enough water for residents in the future.

2. If droughts happen _____ (often), farmers will have to grow crops that need less water.

3. Teenagers often turn to their friends _____ (when there is) stress.

4. _____ high-school students _____ (the largest number of) should go to college in order to prepare for their future.

5. I was really excited because _____ (another time), our university soccer team won the national competition.

6. According to meteorologists, last winter was the coldest _____ (ever).

Use the Vocabulary

Write answers to the following questions. Use the words in bold in your sentences. Then share your answers with a partner.

1. How can you improve your English? Describe **as many** ways **as possible**.

2. Parents **support** their children in many different ways. Give some examples of the different ways they do this.

3. Many students move to a different place when they go to a college. Sometimes parents **are concerned about** their children leaving home. What kind of things **are** they **concerned about**?

4. Who can you **depend on** when you need help? Who helps you **during times of** stress?

5. What kind of exercise do you do **on a regular basis**?

6. Think of a very popular television **series**. Do you ever watch it? What other series have you enjoyed on television?

THINK AND DISCUSS

Work in a small group. Use the information in the reading and your own ideas to discuss the following questions.

1. **Summarize.** Explain in your own words how Meko finds information about past climates.

2. **Connect ideas.** Tree rings are one way to find out about weather in the past. What are some other ways?

3. **Express an opinion.** Do you think Meko's research is important for the world, or just for this area in the United States? Explain your answer.

Vocabulary Review

A Complete the paragraphs with the vocabulary below that you have studied in the unit.

contain chemicals	made an important discovery	as many tree rings as possible
current weather	figure out	supported his research
depend on	a long time ago	

Until recently, scientists thought that 2,000 years ago, England was colder than it is today. However, a German scientist, Jan Esper, _____. Esper wanted to

1
_____ how farmers at that time could grow grapes. He knew farmers grew

2
grapes because there are pictures of this from that time. Yet grapes _____

3
warm weather to grow. If the weather was cooler then, how could farmers grow this fruit 2,000 years ago?

Esper studied _____ from forests in northern Europe. He discovered that

4
_____, northern Europe was warmer than it is today, not cooler. In fact, he

5
found that northern England was about 0.6 degrees warmer than _____. Like

6
other scientists, he looked for more information to make sure he was correct. He studied fossils that
still _____ from 2,000 years ago. These fossils _____, so

7   **8**
Esper was more certain. Although the climate was not dramatically different 2,000 years ago, it was a little warmer—warm enough to grow fruit that farmers cannot grow in this area today.

B Compare answers to Exercise A with a partner. Then discuss the following questions.

Scientists often begin their research by asking a question. What question did Esper ask? How did he begin to answer that question?

C Complete the following sentences in a way that shows that you understand the meaning of the words in bold.

1. On a **typical Monday**, I _____.

2. Here are some ways to **conserve water**: _____.

3. Parents of young children **are often concerned about** _____.

4. My favorite soccer team has been losing recently. I hoped they would win yesterday, but **once again**

_____.

D Work with a partner and write four sentences that include any four of the vocabulary items below. You may use any verb tense and make nouns plural if you want.

apartment residents	fall dramatically	on a regular basis
enormous problem	freezing cold	therefore

Connect the Readings

A Use information from Readings 1 and 2 to complete the outlines below. You do not need to write complete sentences. Write only important words and phrases.

Main Idea: Trees provide information about past climates.

A. Wood fossils—Axel Heiberg Island

- contain chemicals—_____

- chemicals give details of _____

B. _____—Colorado River Area

- _____

- normal rainfall—_____

- _____

Main Idea: Scientists use different methods to learn about past climates.

A. Hope Jahren

- worked at the North Pole

- _____

- _____

B. Dave Meko

- works in southwestern U.S.

- _____

- _____

B With a partner or in a small group, compare answers to Exercise A. Then discuss the following questions.

1. What did you learn about past climates?

2. Which area has very a different climate today than in the past?

3. Which area is experiencing the same climate as in the past?

C Discuss the following questions with a partner. Use your understanding of the readings and your own ideas.

1. Hope Jahren discovered that weather is changing. Is the weather changing where you live?

2. What can people in your area do to conserve water?

3. Weather is an important part of lives. Some people check the weather as soon as they wake up. What about you? Do you check the weather? How do you find out about the weather?

Figures made out of trash, created by artist H.A. Schult, stand near the Matterhorn, Switzerland.

Recycling

FOCUS

1. What kinds of things do you or could you recycle?

2. What are creative ways that some people reuse things that other people usually throw away?

107

Academic Vocabulary

to create	to emphasize	labor
critical	flexible	to transform

Multiword Vocabulary

to date	out of necessity
to make a living	to run short of
to make sense	to take advantage of

Reading Preview

A **Preview.** Read the title. Look at the photos and captions on pages 108–111. Then discuss the following questions with a partner.

1. What do you think the title means?

2. What kinds of materials do the businesses use?

3. What do you think of the products? Do you like them? Would you buy one?

B **Topic vocabulary.** The following words appear in Reading 1. Look at the words and answer the questions with a partner.

affordable	logo	riding
company	popular	tire
entrepreneur	product	trend
inner tubes		

1. Which words are connected to business?

2. Which words are connected to bicycles?

3. Which words are related to a product a lot of people like?

C **Predict.** What do you think this reading will be about? Discuss each word in Exercise B and predict how it may relate to the reading.

Every year, we throw away 1 billion tons of garbage. How can we reduce this waste? Perhaps instead of throwing away garbage, we can use it to start a business.

A worker for the company Plastic Works in Jakarta, Indonesia. The company uses many different types of recycled materials to make bags and other products.

From Useless to Useful

FROM USELESS TO USEFUL

People start new businesses for different reasons. Sometimes they have a great idea. Other times, they decide to make a living by doing something they enjoy. For Eli Reich, his business began when someone stole his bike bag. [1]

Reich was an engineer in Seattle. Because he cared about the environment, he biked to work every day. He carried his work and his laptop in a bike bag. When someone took this bag, he tried to buy a new one. But he couldn't find one he liked. So he decided to make his own. Riding a bike every day leads to lots of tire punctures.[1] As a result, he had plenty of used inner tubes in his apartment. Inner tubes are the inside part of a bike tire. They are soft, flexible, and feel like leather. They are also waterproof—all perfect qualities for a bag. [2]

"For Eli Reich, his business began when someone stole his bike bag."

His friends loved his new bag. Soon, his bike bag was in great demand. Reich quit his job, and started his own business—Alchemy Goods. At first, he depended on his friends for inner tubes. But business was good, and he quickly ran short of these tubes. He needed a new supply. So he asked local bike stores to send him used inner tubes instead of throwing them away. To date, he has used over 300,000 inner tubes. Having a good supply of these materials is a critical part of Reich's business. [3]

Each bag uses as many recycled products as possible. The straps, for example, are old car seat belts.[2] Reich's goal is to use 100 percent recycled materials. This is not easy. "It's hard to come up with a product that is endlessly recycled. We're a step ahead, but we're not [4]

---

[1] *punctures:* small holes that something sharp makes in a tire

[2] *seat belt:* a strong belt attached to a car seat that holds a person in the seat

Eli Reich cuts a seatbelt from an old car to make bags for his company, Alchemy Goods.

An Eli Reich bag made from 100% recycled material

perfect." He wants to let his customers know about his goal, so each bag has a number above the company logo. The number gives the percentage of recycled materials in that particular bag.

Reich emphasizes that he uses recycled materials, but he creates high quality products. *Recycling* turns waste[3] into reusable things that are often cheaper than the original product. Companies turn newspapers into paper cups, for example. *Upcycling* transforms waste into a better quality—and more expensive—product than the original product. Alchemy Goods bags are not cheap. Each bag is handmade. Using recycled materials keeps the cost down, but labor is expensive. "The big challenge is . . . to make the prices affordable," Reich says. Each bag sells for around $130. 5

Creating a business out of other people's trash is a growing trend. Upcycling is becoming popular. Reich joins thousands of small business owners who are taking advantage of the 250 million tons of trash that Americans throw away every year. Like other entrepreneurs, Reich believes this makes sense for business and the environment. 6

---

[3] *waste:* used material that is no longer wanted

READING COMPREHENSION

Big Picture

A Read the following statements. Check (✓) the four statements that express the main ideas of Reading 1.

_____ **1.** Someone stole Reich's bike bag.

_____ **2.** Reich uses as many recycled materials as possible to make bags.

_____ **3.** When more and more people wanted a bag, Reich started his own business.

_____ **4.** In the beginning, friends supplied inner tubes to Reich.

_____ **5.** Each bag has a number.

_____ **6.** Reich finds it difficult to keep the price of his bags affordable.

_____ **7.** Using trash to make good quality products helps business and the environment.

_____ **8.** Americans throw away 250 million tons of trash each year.

B Complete the statement below to express the main idea of the *whole* reading.

Reich's company makes _____ out of _____

and as many other _____ as possible.

Close-Up

Choose the best answer for each of the following questions, according to the reading.

1. Which statement is correct, according to the reading?
   a. Reich asked his friends to help him make his first bag.
   b. Reich had a lot of inner tubes available because he often got tire punctures.
   c. Reich had always wanted to start his own business.
   d. Reich went to his local bike store to get the materials for his first bag.

2. The reading does not explain why bike store owners gave used inner tubes to Alchemy Goods. Why do you think they agreed to do this?
   a. The owners liked the Alchemy Goods bags, but thought they were expensive.
   b. Reich had friends in every local bike store.
   c. People who sell bikes usually prefer to recycle materials.
   d. Alchemy Goods paid a lot of money for the recycled inner tubes.

3. Which statement is *not* correct, according to the reading?
   a. Some bags use more recycled materials than other bags.
   b. Reich lets his customers know how many recycled products he uses for each bag.
   c. The company has not yet reached its goal of using 100 percent recycled products.
   d. Each bag that is produced by Alchemy Goods has the same number above the logo.

4. Why is it difficult to keep the cost of Alchemy Goods bags down?
   a. Recycled materials such as seat belts and inner tubes are expensive.
   b It costs a lot of money to pay people to make each bag.
   c. Not many people want to buy these bags, so the price must be high.
   d. It is difficult to find enough recycled materials to keep producing the bags.

5. Why do you think more small business owners are using recycled products? More than one answer is correct.
   a. It is easy to make a product completely out of recycled materials.
   b. Customers often like to buy products that contain recycled materials.
   c. There is a lot of trash available that businesses can recycle.
   d. It keeps down the cost of labor so the product can be cheaper.

Reading Skill

Understanding Gerund Subjects

Every sentence has a subject. It is important to identify the subject in order to understand the sentence.

Some sentences use a gerund as a subject. A gerund is the base + -*ing* form of a verb. It acts as a noun. It can be a single word or a group of words (a gerund phrase). Look at these examples from Reading 1.

> **Recycling** *turns waste into reusable things that are often cheaper than the original product.*

> **Riding a bike every day** *leads to lots of tire punctures.*

In order to identify gerund subjects, you should

- look for a base + -*ing* form of a verb
- find its verb (Note that gerund subjects always take the singular form of a verb.)

A Read the following sentences. Some contain gerund subjects; some do not. Find and underline the gerund subjects and circle their verbs.

1. Recycling old glass bottles into beautiful art is good business for a company in Liverpool, England.

2. Cleaning these bottles is the first step in the process.

3. The company is working hard to use environmentally friendly chemicals to make the art.

4. Transforming this trash takes a lot of time and skill.

5. After long, careful work, the old bottles are turned into beautiful, colored windows.

B Reread Reading 1. Find any gerund subjects and their verbs. Write them in the chart below and give the paragraph number. The first one is done for you.

	Gerund Subject	Verb
1. Par. 2	Riding a bike every day	leads
2.		
3.		
4.		
5.		

VOCABULARY PRACTICE

Academic Vocabulary

A Find the words in the box in Reading 1. Use the context and the words in parentheses to help you choose the correct word to complete each of the following sentences.

flexible (Par. 2)	emphasizes (Par. 5)	transforms (Par. 5)
critical (Par. 3)	creates (Par. 5)	labor (Par. 5)

1. Californian artist Terry Berlier _____ (turns) street trash into very expensive pieces of art.

2. Having a good idea is a _____ (very important) part of starting your own business.

3. The cost of _____ (workers) is often lower in developing countries.

4. German artist HA Schult _____ (makes) statues of people out of everyday trash. These "people" are everywhere—from the Pyramids in Egypt to the Great Wall of China.

5. The business owner _____ (strongly says) to his workers that hard work is as important as good ideas.

6. Being _____ (able to change) is an important skill for employees today.

B Match the words in bold to words that they typically combine with. Write the letter on the line.

1. to **transform** (something) _____   a. hours, schedule

2. to **create** _____   b. the importance of, the need for

3. **flexible** _____   c. costs, force

4. **critical** _____   d. into, from . . . to

5. to **emphasize** _____   e. jobs, opportunities

6. **labor** _____   f. role in, part of

C The words in bold below show the academic words and the words they often appear with from Exercise B. Complete the sentences with your own words.

1. Teachers **emphasize the need for** _____ .

2. _____ is a **critical part of** being a successful college student.

3. When the company started to pay health insurance, its **labor costs** _____ .

4. Parents like **flexible schedules** because _____ .

5. A group of business people **transformed** the old part of the city **into** _____ .

6. The city government is trying to **create jobs** for young people because _____ .

Multiword Vocabulary

A Find the multiword vocabulary in bold in Reading 1. Use the context to help you understand the meaning. Then match each item to the correct definition.

_____ 1. **to make a living** (Par. 1)   a. is sensible

_____ 2. **out of necessity** (Par. 1)   b. did not have enough of something

_____ 3. **ran short of** (Par. 3)   c. using as an opportunity

_____ 4. **to date** (Par. 3)   d. due to need

_____ 5. **taking advantage of** (Par. 6)   e. to earn money to support yourself

_____ 6. **makes sense** (Par. 6)   f. up to the present time

B Complete the following sentences with the correct multiword vocabulary from Exercise A.

1. James didn't want to ride his bike to work every day. He did it _____ because he couldn't afford a car.

2. I worked part-time in a restaurant when I was in college. I enjoyed it so much that I decided _____ by working in restaurants and hotels.

3. When the recycling company _____ of old newspapers, it had to start using different kinds of old paper.

4. _____ , city residents have been able to recycle about half of their trash. The city leaders hope recycling will increase even more by the end of next year.

5. The cost of gas is increasing, so it _____ for the city to use electric buses.

6. A popular clothing store has reduced its prices by 50 percent. Many customers are _____ these low prices. As a result, the store is very crowded.

Use the Vocabulary

Write answers to the following questions. Use the words in bold in your answers. Then share your answers with a partner.

1. Schools and colleges usually have libraries to help students find information and succeed in class. What other resources can you **take advantage of** in your school?

2. How do you plan **to make a living** when you graduate from school?

3. Your English teacher asks you to write two paragraphs about your city. You have finished one, but you have **run short of** ideas. What do you do?

4. What jobs have **flexible schedules**? Would you like this kind of work schedule?

5. Some high schools **emphasize** the importance of non-academic subjects such as sports, music, and the arts. Do you think this is a good idea?

6. Speaking is a **critical part of** learning English. Sometimes, however, it is difficult to get enough practice. What do you do to practice speaking?

7. Studying overseas can be expensive, so does it **make sense** to do this? Why do so many students attend schools outside their home countries?

8. How many college classes have you taken **to date**? What classes do you plan to take in the future?

THINK AND DISCUSS

Work in a small group. Use the information in the reading and your own ideas to discuss the following questions.

1. Summarize. Explain how the Alchemy Goods company started.

2. Evaluate. How has this company become successful?

3. Relate to personal experience. Do you recycle some of your trash at home? What about at school or at work? How easy is it to recycle trash in your community?

4. Express an opinion. Do you think governments should encourage more use of recycled products? How can a government do this?

READING 2

Academic Vocabulary

accommodations	mobile	a shortage
construction	a project	spacious

Multiword Vocabulary

affordable housing	to make use of something
to come equipped with	to pile up
in other words	to think outside the box

Reading Preview

A **Preview.** Read the title of Reading 2 and the first sentence of each paragraph on pages 118–119. Check (✓) five topics that you think might be in this reading.

_____ **1.** Employment opportunities in Europe

_____ **2.** Amsterdam

_____ **3.** Reusing shipping containers

_____ **4.** Creative ideas

_____ **5.** Life in small cities

_____ **6.** Different ways to use containers

_____ **7.** The cost of education in Europe

_____ **8.** Finding solutions to problems

B **Topic vocabulary.** The following words appear in Reading 2. Look at the words and answer the questions with a partner.

container	imagination	solution
creatively	impossible	steel
crowded	original idea	worried
ideal		

1. What is a "container"? Which word describes the material used to make a container?

2. Which adjectives relate to problems?

3. Which words are about solving a problem?

C **Predict.** What do you think this reading will be about? Discuss each word in Exercise B and predict how it may relate to the reading.

Apartments made from used shipping containers at Trinity Buoy Wharf in London, England

Would you like to live in a box? This is where many students in Amsterdam now live. Find out more about this unusual kind of student housing.

Living in a BOX

LIVING IN A BOX

Student Rose Mandungu, who lives in a shipping container in Amsterdam, Netherlands

A problem is only a problem until there is a solution. We find solutions by thinking creatively. We use our imagination and come up with innovative ideas. In other words, we think outside the box. Sometimes, thinking outside the box solves not just one, but two problems. 1

Problem #1

Amsterdam, Netherlands, is one of the most exciting cities in Europe. As a result, it is very crowded. Housing is in great demand and, therefore, very expensive. In particular, there is a shortage of affordable housing for students. Students need low-cost apartments. Finding this type of housing was almost impossible until recently. 2

Problem #2

While Dutch colleges were trying to solve the housing problem, thousands of unused shipping containers were piling up in ports around the world. These huge steel containers transport products from one country to another. One hundred million of them cross the oceans each year. The 3 average life of each container is about 10 years. Steel companies recycle some of the old containers. Yet they can't recycle all of them because there are so many. In fact, there are over two million old containers in ports around the world.

The Solution

Back in the Netherlands, a construction company came up with an original idea. Why not reuse these shipping containers as student housing? The containers are ideal for building. They are all the same size and fit together like a giant LEGO[1] set. The steel is strong. Moreover, these containers are so widely available that they are quite inexpensive to buy. For all these reasons, you can use them to build apartments quickly and cheaply.

"Student housing is just one use for old shipping containers."

Finding a new use for these shipping containers has another important advantage. It takes a lot of energy to recycle the materials in the container. However, it takes very little energy to reuse the containers for housing. For all these reasons, in Amsterdam it made sense to build with them. So, the city organized the Keetwonen project. Building began in 2005, and after only a few weeks, hundreds of Amsterdam students had new homes.

When students first heard about this project, many were worried. They thought the container apartments would be small, noisy, and cold. However, they were impressed when they saw them. Compared to other student accommodations, each apartment is quite spacious. It has a kitchen, bedroom with a study area, and a bathroom. Large windows let in light. Each apartment has its own balcony. The apartments are warm and quiet. They come equipped with a high-speed Internet connection. Living in a shipping container has become very popular. Today, over 3,000 students live in the Keetwonen container village.

Final Thoughts

Student housing is just one use for old shipping containers. Since the Keetwonen project, architects are making good use of these steel boxes in many ways. There are container homes in Canada and the United States. Odessa, Ukraine, has a huge container shopping mall. In other cities, there are container offices, restaurants, and coffee shops. They are even used as mobile health clinics. Clearly, finding new uses for these containers is a solution to more than one problem.

---

[1] *LEGO:* a company trademark name for children's building toys using special plastic bricks that fit together

READING COMPREHENSION

Big Picture

A Choose the answer that best completes each of the following sentences.

1. The reading discusses _____.
   a. one problem
   b. two specific problems

2. According to the reading, _____ in Amsterdam.
   a. student housing is difficult to find
   b. people do not enjoy living in Amsterdam

3. The number of old shipping containers _____ in ports throughout the world.
   a. is increasing
   b. is decreasing

4. There are _____ reasons why shipping containers are perfect materials for building.
   a. two
   b. four

5. At first, many students were _____ the container apartments.

    a. concerned about   **b.** happy with

6. Building companies are transforming shipping containers into _____.

    a. only student housing   **b.** different construction projects

7. Using containers to build student housing is an example of _____.

    a. one solution that solves several problems   **b.** two solutions that solve one problem

B Work with a partner or in a small group. Write a sentence that expresses the main idea of the *whole* reading.

_____

Close-Up

A Decide which of the following statements are true or false according to the reading. Write *T* (True) or *F* (False) next to each one.

_____ **1.** An innovative idea means thinking in traditional ways.

_____ **2.** The high cost of housing in Amsterdam makes it difficult for students to find affordable apartments.

_____ **3.** Most containers are no longer used in transportation after a period of 10 years.

_____ **4.** Construction companies recycle all old and used containers.

_____ **5.** The Dutch student housing project took only a short time to complete.

_____ **6.** The container apartments are much smaller than other student housing in Amsterdam.

_____ **7.** The upcycled shipping containers are now in great demand with students in Amsterdam.

_____ **8.** The reading gives the example of shipping container malls in Canada and the United States.

B Work with a partner or in a small group. Change the false sentences in Exercise A to make them true.

Reading Skill

Finding Reasons

Writers provide reasons to explain and support main ideas. Understanding these reasons will help you better understand the main ideas.

When you look for reasons, try to find information that answers the question "Why?"

Example

    Main idea: Shipping containers transform well into apartments. Why?

        Reason 1: They fit together easily.

        Reason 2: The steel is strong.

        Reason 3: They are cheap.

A Read the following main idea statements from Reading 2. Quickly scan the reading to match each main idea to a paragraph. Then read more slowly to find a reason or reasons that support each main idea. Write the answers on the lines.

1. Finding low-cost student housing in Amsterdam used to be difficult. Why?

_____

2. Steel companies cannot recycle every shipping container. Why?

_____

3. Reusing these containers for apartments is good for the environment. Why?

_____

4. Students are impressed with their new housing. Why?

_____

5. Finding a new use for shipping containers is a solution to more than one problem. Why?

_____

VOCABULARY PRACTICE

Academic Vocabulary

A Find the words in bold in Reading 2. Use the context to help you match each word to the correct definition.

_____ **1. shortage** (Par. 2)

_____ **2. construction** (Par. 4)

_____ **3. project** (Par. 5)

_____ **4. accommodations** (Par. 6)

_____ **5. spacious** (Par. 6)

_____ **6. mobile** (Par. 7)

a. able to be moved

b. large

c. housing

d. lack of, not enough

e. building

f. planned piece of work

B Work with a partner to complete the following sentences. Match each academic word in bold with a word in the box that it often appears with.

apartment	collaborative	library	on-campus	serious	site

1. In some parts of the world, there is a(n) _____ **shortage** of fresh, clean water. This leads to many health problems.

2. There used to be a **mobile** _____ where I lived. It was a van full of books, and it came to our neighborhood every Tuesday.

3. It was a(n) _____ **project**—students and teachers worked together to clean up the neighborhood playground.

4. Work at the **construction** _____ stopped after one of the men fell and needed medical care.

5. There are not enough _____ **accommodations**, so students live in apartments outside the university area.

6. The Jacobs family of five was very happy to move into their new, **spacious** _____. This one is much bigger than their previous one.

Multiword Vocabulary

Ⓐ Find the words in the box in Reading 2. Use the context to help you understand the meaning. Then complete the sentences with the multiword vocabulary.

in other words (Par. 1)	piling up (Par. 3)
think outside the box (Par. 1)	come equipped with (Par. 6)
affordable housing (Par. 2)	making good use of something (Par. 7)

1. When you _____, you come up with new and creative solutions.

2. To _____ can mean that useful things such as Internet access, air-conditioning, and a washer and dryer are available in a house or an apartment.

3. We use the phrase _____ to introduce an alternative explanation to something we have just said.

4. _____ means we are taking advantage of something.

5. When something is _____, it means more and more of these things are building up.

6. _____ refers to low-cost houses or apartments that ordinary people can either rent or buy.

Ⓑ Complete the following paragraph with the correct multiword vocabulary from the box.

affordable housing	in other words	piling up
came equipped with	made use of	thinking outside the box

After the 2010 earthquake, the small country of Haiti was in trouble. Thousands of people were killed or badly hurt. Even more lost their homes and their jobs. Haitians needed help fast. Organizations helped the government build _____ because people
                                                                                        1
needed homes. Life started to get a little better, but basic city services were not available. As trash was _____ in the streets, Haitians started to get sick. The doctors
         2
and nurses needed more health clinics. An organization called Containers to Clinics (C2C) decided to help. This company transforms shipping containers into medical clinics. For Haiti, C2C _____ volunteers to keep the cost down. Each clinic
      3
_____ fresh water and electricity. Because they were mobile, the
      4
clinics could move to where people really needed help. These container clinics were practical solutions to the serious problems caused by the earthquake. _____,
                                                                            5
these clinics were the result of _____.
                                  6

Use the Vocabulary

Write answers to the following questions. Use the words in bold in your answers. Then share your answers with a partner.

1. What sort of **accommodations** do you live in right now? Is it an apartment? A home? Student housing? Is it **spacious** or small?

2. When you first moved into your present living space, what did it **come equipped with** in terms of appliances? Did it have a stove, for example?

3. People use their **mobile** phones for many reasons other than making a call. What do you use your phone for?

4. Think about your teachers in high school. Did they encourage you to **think outside the box**? Explain your answer.

5. In many cities, only very wealthy people can afford to live near the city center. Is **affordable housing** hard to find in your city?

6. Many companies are **making use of** recycled products these days. Can you think of an example of this type of product?

7. In some countries, there is a **serious shortage** of openings in university programs. As a result, many students have to go to another state or country in order to attend university. Is this the situation in your country?

THINK AND DISCUSS

Work in a small group. Use the information in the reading and your own ideas to discuss the following questions.

1. **Summarize.** What are the advantages of converting shipping containers into apartments, shops, and medical clinics?

2. **Express an opinion.** Do you like the Dutch apartments? Is there anything you don't like about these designs?

3. **Identify solutions.** Some companies are turning shipping containers into apartments. However, there are still thousands of old containers in ports. Can you think of other ways we could use these steel containers?

4. **Apply knowledge.** Imagine you work in a construction company. You are working on a project to convert a 40-by-8-foot container into a mobile library. Think about what a good library should come equipped with. Draw a design that shows your finished container library.

Vocabulary Review

A Complete the paragraphs with the vocabulary below that you have studied in the unit.

construction site	labor force	make use of	to date
creates more jobs	made his living	spacious	widely available

In 1957, Nek Chand _____
1
by building roads in northern India. At times, this
part of the country looked like a huge

_____. The government was
2
building a whole new city—Chandigarh. Chand
worked hard during the day, but when the other
workers went home, he disappeared into the
forest. There he built beautiful statues and pieces
of art. He built his art from trash that was

_____ because of all the
3
construction. He did this every night for many
years. And no one knew about it.

Examples of Nek Chand's statues in Chandargh, India

In 1976, the government discovered his secret
art garden. By this time, it covered a large part of
the forest and it contained thousands of statues.
The government wanted to destroy it, but local
residents encouraged the government to create a
public park. The government agreed and provided
a _____ of 50 workers to help
4
Chand with his work. The garden now employs many people, and each year it

_____ for local workers. It is now a _____ area of over
5   6
25 acres. There are 5,000 pieces of art. Chand and his team continue to _____
7
everyday trash by transforming it into art. _____, over 12 million visitors
8
have enjoyed this unusual trash garden.

B Compare answers to Exercise A with a partner. Then discuss the following questions.

*Does Nek Chand's trash garden seem an interesting place to visit? What public art is in
your community?*

C Complete the following sentences in a way that shows that you understand the
meaning of the words in bold.

1. My teacher **emphasizes the need for** _____.

2. In some cities, there is a **serious shortage** of _____.

3. I am **running short of** money, so I must _____.

4. Tomas worked hard to **transform** the old, dark apartment **into** a _____.

D Work with a partner and write four sentences that include any four of the vocabulary items below. You may use any verb tense and make nouns plural if you want.

make sense	on-campus accommodations	take advantage of
mobile library	spacious apartment	think outside the box

Connect the Readings

A In Readings 1 and 2, the writer explains why some things provide good materials for recycling. Look back at both readings to find examples and reasons that support the following statements. Use these reasons to complete the chart. The first one is done for you.

Statement	Reading 1	Reading 2
Some materials are widely available.	*Inner tubes—people are always getting punctures.*	
Some materials are perfect to make into more expensive products.		
Recycled products are often in great demand.		
Companies can recycle one thing into different products.		
Recycling is good for the environment.		
Recycling is good for business.		

B With a partner or in a small group, compare answers to Exercise A. Then discuss the following questions.

1. Do you agree that people like to buy products that use recycled materials? Do you buy these products?

2. Readings 1 and 2 suggest that recycling is good for the environment. However, they do not give many reasons for this statement. Why do you think recycling helps our planet?

3. Can you think of a large business that recycles a lot of its products?

C Discuss the following questions with a partner. Use your understanding of the readings and your own ideas.

1. What kinds of products can you recycle where you live?

2. If recycling is good for the environment, how can schools encourage students to recycle more?

Wildlife
RESCUE

A wildlife rescue worker puts a sea turtle in a box at the Audubon Nature Center in New Orleans, Louisiana, USA.

FOCUS

1. What do you think this woman is doing? Why?

2. The world's population keeps growing. What problems can this cause for the world's wild animals?

Academic Vocabulary

to expand	to interact	to release
extensive	a process	urbanization

Multiword Vocabulary

to get used to	on the black market
to go for	step-by-step
to leave behind	to take turns

Reading Preview

A **Preview.** Read the title and look at the photos on pages 128–130. Then discuss the following questions with a partner or in a small group.

1. What are people at the wildlife center trying to do?

2. Why do you think there is a need for this center?

3. How can the keepers help the elephants?

B **Topic vocabulary.** The following words appear in Reading 1. Look at the words and answer the questions with a partner.

center	director	keepers
danger	enemies	kill
deadly	hunters	rescue

1. Which words are most closely connected to an organization that helps animals?

2. Which words describe different kinds of people?

3. Which words explain why elephants need help?

C **Predict.** What do you think this reading will be about? Discuss each word in Exercise B and predict how it may relate to the reading.

A baby elephant is alone. His mother is dead. He is hungry and weak. Read about what happens to him and other baby elephants in Kenya.

Saving Baby Elephants

A keeper at a wildlife center in the Nairobi National Park, Kenya, walks with a group of baby elephants.

Mishak Nzimbi rubs his eyes as he 1 prepares the bottle of warm milk. Like other people taking care of babies, he is exhausted. It is 5:30 a.m., and he hasn't had much sleep. He speaks to the three-month-old gently, offers the bottle, and smiles as she starts drinking. At 400 pounds (181 kilos), the baby is too heavy to hold. So Nzimbi sits next to his African elephant and makes sure she finishes her breakfast.

Nzimbi is the head keeper at an elephant 2 rescue center in Kenya. Unfortunately, many elephants in this country need rescuing. They face two enemies: hunters and urbanization. Hunters kill elephants for their tusks.[1] This is illegal, but hunters know that tusks go for a lot of money on the black market. Urbanization is equally deadly for these magnificent animals. As villages and cities expand, forest land decreases. People build homes and plant fields where elephants used to live. Hungry elephants then wander[2] into villages and farms looking for food. They often cause extensive damage, so farmers kill them.

> *"Unfortunately, many elephants in this country need rescuing. They face two enemies: hunters and urbanization."*

When hunters or farmers kill adult elephants, 3 they often leave behind baby elephants. When a baby elephant loses its mother, its life is also in great danger. This is because it depends on its mother's milk for about four years. Without this milk, the baby has little chance of survival. Loss of a mother also leads to sadness. Research shows that elephants, like people, feel emotions. If the mother elephant dies, the baby elephant grieves[3] and often becomes ill. This is when the elephant rescue center helps out.

The center's goal is to raise young elephants 4 and release them back to the wild. This is a complicated process. So the center takes a step-by-step approach. First, the keepers take turns looking after the baby elephants. They do not want an elephant to become too attached to[4] one of the keepers. Each morning, a baby meets its keeper for that day. Then the keepers take the elephants into the forest. This is a critical part of the process. The elephants learn how to eat in the wild.[5] They also learn how to interact with each other. When an elephant is about four and no

---

[1] *tusks:* an elephant's two very long, curved teeth
[2] *wander:* walk around an area with no particular purpose

[3] *grieves:* feels great sadness about a death
[4] *attached to:* like someone very much; dependent on
[5] *in the wild:* in natural areas not used by people

longer needs milk, it is a "teenager." The keepers move it to an area 100 miles (160.1 kilometers) away. Here, the teenage elephants are allowed to go alone into the forest and meet wild elephants. They become more independent. Keepers encourage them to have "sleepovers"[6] in the forest. The teenagers often go out for days at a time, but then return to the keepers. It often takes eight to ten years for an elephant to get used to living in the wild.

Today, Nzimbi is taking care of a new arrival to 5 the center. This baby elephant was with his mother when hunters killed her. He is nervous and sad. He communicates his sadness and fear by crying.

_____

[6] *sleepover:* when a child spends the night at a
    friend's house

As the other babies hear him, they immediately go over to him. "Whenever we get a new baby here, the others will come around and lovingly put their trunks[7] on its back to comfort it," explains Daphne Sheldrick, the center's director. "They have such big hearts." By evening, the new baby is following the others and looks a little happier.

At bedtime, Nzimbi lies down with his baby 6 elephant. "We have to sleep with them because when we leave them, they cry," Nzimbi explains. Does he need an alarm clock to wake up for the feedings? "Oh, no," he says. "Every three hours you feel a trunk reach up and pull your blanket off. The elephants are our alarms."

_____

[7] *trunks:* the long noses of elephants

READING COMPREHENSION

Big Picture

Choose the statement that best completes each of the following sentences.

1. The main idea of paragraph 1 is that _____ .
   a. Nzimbi is exhausted because he didn't get enough sleep
   b. the baby elephant weighs 400 pounds
   c. Nzimbi has to feed a baby elephant all through the night

2. The main idea of paragraph 2 is that elephants _____ .
   a. are often killed when they wander into farms and cause damage
   b. are hunted for their valuable ivory tusks
   c. face danger from both hunters and the spread of cities

3. The main idea of paragraph 3 is that a baby elephant _____ .
   a. needs its mother's milk for four years
   b. has little chance of survival if it loses its mother
   c. shows emotions just like a human baby

4. The main idea of paragraph 4 is that _____ .
   a. raising and releasing elephants into the wild is a long and complicated process
   b. raising elephants begins when the baby elephants are very young
   c. baby elephants have to learn how to survive in the forest and to live with other elephants

5. The main idea of paragraph 5 is that _____ .
   a. the newest arrival at the center is a male elephant
   b. Nzimbi's baby elephant is very nervous
   c. the new baby elephant is comforted by the other baby elephants

6. The main idea of the whole reading is _____ .
   a. baby elephants cannot survive without help from the center
   b. hunters and farmers are killing elephants in Kenya
   c. elephants have less land because cities are spreading into forest areas

Close-Up

A Scan Reading 1 to find answers to the following questions. Write the answers on the lines.

1. Why do farmers sometimes kill elephants? _____

2. Why can't hunters sell elephant tusks in regular stores? _____

3. How long does a baby elephant depend on its mother's milk? _____

4. In what ways are baby elephants like people? _____

5. What two skills do baby elephants learn in the forest? _____

6. By the end of the day, how is the new elephant's behavior different, according to paragraph 5?

   _____

7. How often do baby elephants need a bottle of milk during the night? _____

B Compare answers to Exercise A with a partner. If your answers are different, go back to the reading to find the correct answer.

Reading Skill

Improving Reading Speed

You sometimes need to read quickly to get the main idea of a reading or to complete a test. So, reading quickly is an important skill. Like any skill, you can improve your speed by practicing.

These strategies will help you increase your reading speed:

- Choose a reading you have already read.
- Read the title and look at the pictures to remind yourself of the topic.
- Don't move your finger under the words or speak the words as you read—this slows you down.
- If you come to an unfamiliar word, don't stop. You don't have to understand every word in order to understand the reading.
- Try to read as quickly as you can.
- Practice regularly. Time yourself as you practice.

A Read the following paragraph quickly. Do not stop for unfamiliar words. Then answer the question below about the main idea. Are you able to get the main idea when you read quickly?

South African Lawrence Anthony was known as the Elephant Whisperer. He had an amazing ability to work with elephants. He worked with terrified and violent elephants, and he learned how to calm them down. On one occasion, a herd of elephants in the north of the country was behaving very aggressively. Hunters had killed their leader. The government was going to shoot the herd because the elephants were so dangerous. Anthony solved the problem by moving the elephants to his land. He then spent years getting to know these dangerous elephants. They learned to trust him, and they calmed down. Amazingly, when Anthony died in March 2012, this same herd of elephants walked for 12 hours to his house. They stayed there for two days to say good-bye to the man who had saved them. How did they know? That's a mystery we still do not understand.

What is the main idea of this paragraph?
- **a.** Anthony was called the Elephant Whisperer.
- **b.** South African Lawrence Anthony took care of elephants at his farm.
- **c.** Anthony had an amazing ability to interact with elephants.
- **d.** Elephants came to say good-bye when Anthony died.

B Now time yourself. Read the paragraph about Lawrence Anthony again for ten seconds. After ten seconds, stop and write the number *1* where you stop. Then read it again for ten seconds, starting at the beginning of the paragraph. Write the number *2* where you stop. You should see that you were able to read more quickly the second time.

C Follow the strategies in the skill box and reread Reading 1. Read for 30 seconds. Write the number *1* where you stop. Repeat this activity once more. Write the number *2*. You should see that by practicing, you are increasing your reading speed.

VOCABULARY PRACTICE

Academic Words

A Find the words in bold in Reading 1. Use the context and the sentences below to help you match each word to the correct definition.

1. **Urbanization** (Par. 2) puts pressure on wild animals because as cities get bigger, the land for animals gets smaller.
   a. a strong economy   **b.** the spread of buildings and houses

2. During difficult economic times, more animals need help, so rescue centers try to **expand** (Par. 2) their services to care for more animals.
   a. increase the size of   **b.** make something cheaper

3. The university has done **extensive** (Par. 2) research on how chimpanzees communicate. This has helped scientists understand these intelligent animals.
   a. some   **b.** a lot of

4. The goal of the Wildlife Center is to nurse wild animals back to health and then **release** (Par. 4) them into the wild.
   a. follow   **b.** set them free

5. When the keepers released the dolphin into the wild, they watched very carefully to make sure that it could **interact** (Par 4) comfortably with the other dolphins.
   a. eat   **b.** communicate, spend time with

6. It was a long and complicated **process** (Par. 4) to save birds and other marine animals after oil spilled into the ocean.
   a. series of actions   **b.** journey

B The words and phrases in the box often appear with the academic words in bold. Complete the sentences with the correct word or phrase.

creative	experience	into	rapid	results	with others

1. Many cities in the world are experiencing _____ **urbanization**. This is happening so quickly that many people cannot find accommodations when they first move to a city.

2. Young children have to learn how to **interact** _____. They must learn how to talk to, listen to, and behave with people.

3. Writing children's books is a very _____ **process**. You need a lot of good ideas and imagination.

4. The university **released** the _____ of its study. This study found that students are more successful in college if they have good friends and if they are happy.

5. The British company now wants to **expand** _____ Asia, so it is setting up offices in China and Vietnam.

6. The new director of the zoo has **extensive** _____ in working with African animals—she worked in a South African zoo for 10 years.

Multiword Vocabulary

A Find the multiword vocabulary in bold in Reading 1. Then use the context to help you understand the meaning. Then match each item to the correct definition.

_____	**1. go for** (Par. 2)	**a.**	not take something with you
_____	**2. on the black market** (Par. 2)	**b.**	one stage at a time
_____	**3. leave behind** (Par. 3)	**c.**	become accustomed to something
_____	**4. step-by-step** (Par. 4)	**d.**	do something one person after the other
_____	**5. take turns** (Par. 4)	**e.**	a place to buy and sell things illegally
_____	**6. get used to** (Par. 4)	**f.**	be sold for an amount of money

B Complete the following sentences with the correct multiword vocabulary from Exercise A.

1. When hunters kill the leader of a herd, they _____ a very frightened and confused group of elephants.

2. When wild animals first arrive at a zoo, it takes a while for them to _____ living in a cage. After a week or so, most animals are more comfortable in a zoo.

3. The baby tiger needs feeding every two hours, so the keepers _____ staying up at night to do this. Each keeper takes night duty a few times a week.

4. If people stopped buying illegal animal products _____, illegal hunting would decrease.

5. When you first learn to do something complicated, you should take a

_____ approach. This will make it easier.

6. Unfortunately, wild animals such as tigers and panda bears

_____ a lot of money, so hunters keep trying to catch them.

Use the Vocabulary

Write answers to the following questions. Use the words in bold in your answers. Then share your answers with a partner.

1. Everyone agrees that students need to **expand** their vocabulary when they are learning a new language. What are some of the best ways of doing this? How are you trying to expand your English vocabulary?

2. Think about something you are good at doing. Perhaps it is cooking a special dish or fixing the engine of a car. Using a **step-by-step** approach, explain exactly how to do this.

3. Have you ever **left** something important **behind** while you are travelling such as your cell phone or passport? What happened?

4. Think of an area you know well. What effect is **rapid urbanization** having on this area?

5. Most cultures have specific ideas about how young people should **interact with** older people. Give an example from your culture.

6. How much do mobile phones **go for**? Is it worth paying a lot of money for an expensive phone?

7. What kinds of products do people sell **on the black market**? Do the police try to stop this?

8. Think back to a time when you moved from one school to another school. Was it difficult **to get used to** the new school? Did you have to make new friends, for example?

THINK AND DISCUSS

Work in a small group. Use the information in the reading and your own ideas to discuss the following questions.

1. Summarize. Why are Kenyan elephants in danger?

2. Use what you know. Reading 1 discusses how urbanization affects elephants. Cities are growing everywhere. This almost always affects many kinds of animals. For example, in the United States, coyotes (wild, doglike animals) now live in urban areas. How is urbanization affecting animals in your country?

3. Express an opinion. Can governments stop animals such as elephants from being killed by hunters? Do you think the only future for these animals is in zoos?

Academic Vocabulary

despite	to limit	to monitor
habitat	a location	an occurrence

Multiword Vocabulary

all kinds of	to be at stake
to arrive at the scene	foster care
at an alarming rate	to go about

A three-year-old female koala looks out from a tree in a town in Queensland, Australia.

Reading Preview

A **Preview.** Read the title of the reading and the first two sentences of each paragraph on pages 138–139. Look at the photos on pages 136–138. Check (✓) three topics that you think might be in this reading.

_____ **1.** Effects of urbanization on eucalyptus trees

_____ **2.** Life for koalas in zoos

_____ **3.** The role of volunteers in protecting koalas

_____ **4.** How koalas live in the wild

_____ **5.** Financial problems of the Australian government

_____ **6.** How the government can help koalas

Everyone loves the Australian koala. But it is in real danger. What is happening to these animals? Find out and meet the people who are trying to help them.

B **Topic vocabulary.** The following words appear in Reading 2. Look at the words and answer the questions with a partner.

creature	fierce	species
cuddly	snarls	suburbs
dispatcher	specialist	urban areas
downtown		

1. Which words explain the areas where this reading takes place?

2. Which words are connected to animals?

3. Which words describe job positions?

C **Predict.** What do you think this reading will be about? Discuss each word in Exercise B and predict how it may relate to the reading.

Koalas
in
Parking Lots

After a car hits a male koala in Queensland, Australia, a rescue worker carries him to safety.

Lions in downtown Nairobi? Baboons[1] in the middle of Cape Town? People expect an exciting life in the city. They don't expect to come face-to-face with a wild animal. Yet this is an increasingly common occurrence in many cities. As urban areas grow, animal habitats disappear. As a result, all kinds of animals move into the cities looking for food. Unfortunately, this human–animal interaction is often deadly—for the animal.

In cities across Australia, people are likely to see koalas in downtown areas. In fact, city residents are getting used to seeing koalas in their backyards. As cities grow and suburbs spread, koala habitat has turned into parking lots and shopping malls. This is not good news. Cars and dogs, in particular, have not been kind to this animal. They kill many koalas. In the past few years, koala numbers have declined at an alarming rate.

Volunteers are stepping in to try to protect this species from the deadly effects of

"In the past few years, koala numbers have declined at an alarming rate."

urbanization. One of these volunteers is Megan Aitken, a resident of Brisbane. When the phone rings in the middle of the night, she knows what to do. The caller gives her the location, and within minutes, she is out the door.

When Aitken arrives at the scene, she finds a koala is stuck in a chain-link fence. Despite their cuddly appearance, koalas are fierce. So Aitken puts on heavy leather gloves and carefully frees the koala from the fence. She drops it into a cage. The koala snarls and snaps. It's terrified.

Koalas survive by feeding on eucalyptus trees. Each koala also has its own territory, or space. So Aitken must release this one in a nearby eucalyptus tree. "This is the whole problem," she says. "There are so few places left for the koala." In the dark, she drives a short way and frees the koala. It quickly climbs a tree and disappears. "Good luck, little one," Aitken says.

Deidré de Villiers knows that koalas need more than luck to survive. She is a koala specialist. She studies koalas by day, and at

---

[1] *baboons:* large monkeys with long faces

night, she takes her job home with her. Her living room is equipped with baskets for the babies and cages for the teenagers. Over the years, she has provided foster care to over 60 koalas, nursing them back to health. Then, like Aitken, she releases them and hopes they survive.

De Villiers believes that the government 7 needs to do more to protect this creature. She has a clear idea of how to go about doing this.

She thinks the government should first monitor koala numbers to get more accurate information. Then, she argues, the government must limit new construction in koala habitat. This will give the koala population a chance to increase again. Until this happens, however, de Villiers and Aitken will no doubt wake up to more midnight phone calls. And they will do this willingly. After all, the future of this much loved species is at stake.

READING COMPREHENSION

Big Picture

A Choose the statement that best completes each of the following sentences.

1. The main idea of paragraph 1 is that _____ .
   a. people move to cities because they want an exciting life
   b. more and more people are seeing wild animals in downtown areas
   c. there are baboons in downtown Cape Town

2. The main idea of paragraph 2 is that _____ .
   a. urbanization has led to koalas living in cities
   b. the number of koalas is falling because of the growth of cities
   c. cars often hit and kill koalas, and dogs hurt them

3. The main idea of paragraph 3 is that _____ .
   a. a dispatcher calls volunteers at night
   b. Megan Aitken lives in Brisbane
   c. volunteers work hard to help koalas

4. The main idea of paragraph 4 is that _____ .
   a. koalas are cute, but fierce
   b. Aitken frees the koala from the fence
   c. the koala snaps at Aitken

5. The main idea of paragraph 5 is that _____ .
   a. Aitken is worried that there is not enough space left for koalas
   b. koalas eat and sleep in eucalyptus trees
   c. Aitken releases the koala near its own tree so that it can survive

6. The main idea of paragraph 6 is that _____ .
   a. de Villiers is a friend of Megan Aitken
   b. de Villiers looks after koalas in her home
   c. de Villiers loves koalas

7. The main idea of paragraph 7 is that _____ .
   a. de Villiers believes that the government should find out more about the koala population and limit building in koala habitat
   b. de Villiers knows what to do because she is an expert on koalas and has worked with this creature for many years
   c. volunteers like de Villiers and Aitken must continue to work hard to save this species

B Every author has a purpose for writing a text. Read the list below and check (✓) the author's purpose for writing Reading 2.

_____ **1.** To explain how koalas live in Australia

_____ **2.** To encourage the Australian government to do more to help koalas

_____ **3.** To explain why koalas are in serious need of protection

_____ **4.** To show that volunteers work very hard to protect this species

Close-Up

A Decide which of the following statements are true or false according to the reading. Write *T* (True) or *F* (False) next to each one.

_____ **1.** Visitors to Cape Town expect to see baboons in the center of the city.

_____ **2.** It is becoming common for dogs to kill koalas.

_____ **3.** The number of koalas has risen in recent years.

_____ **4.** It is unusual for Aitken to have to rescue a koala in the middle of the night.

_____ **5.** Koalas can bite and scratch, so volunteers have to take care.

_____ **6.** Aitken drives a long way before she releases the koala.

_____ **7.** Koalas feed on several different types of trees.

_____ **8.** De Villiers looks after healthy koalas of all ages.

_____ **9.** The Australian government has an accurate idea of how many koalas live in the wild today.

_____ **10.** De Villiers believes the government needs to limit new construction in areas where koalas live naturally.

B Work with a partner or in a small group. Change the false statements in Exercise A to make them true.

Reading Skill

Identifying Reporting Verbs

In academic writing, a writer often uses information from experts. This information supports the writer's ideas. Writers use reporting verbs to introduce information from other people.

There are many reporting verbs in English, and they introduce different kinds of information. For example, sometimes a reporting verb introduces a fact—something that is true. Other times, it introduces an opinion—something someone believes. Look at the following sentences:

> Jane Goodall's work with chimpanzees **proves** that this animal is intelligent. (fact)

> After a lifetime of working with wild animals, Goodall **believes** that the world must do more to protect them in their habitats. (opinion)

Reporting verbs that introduce facts: *explain, show, find, prove, illustrate, say, learn*

Reporting verbs that introduce opinions: *believe, think, claim, argue*

A Read the following sentences about Jane Goodall. Underline the reporting verbs. Circle the facts or opinions they introduce.

1. After living in the forest with chimpanzees for several years, Goodall learned that these animals communicate by using different sounds.

2. She also found that they show emotion—for example, they hug each other.

3. Goodall thinks that African countries should spend more money on protecting chimpanzees from hunters.

4. She believes that people should not keep these animals as pets because they are wild animals and are happier in their natural habitat.

5. Goodall also argues that scientists should not use chimpanzees for medical research.

B Reread Reading 2. As you read, complete the following steps.

1. Underline reporting verbs.

2. Circle the person who is providing this information.

3. Decide if the information is fact or opinion. In the margin, write *F* for fact and *O* for opinion.

C Compare answers to Exercise B with a partner. Discuss any answers that are different.

VOCABULARY PRACTICE

Academic Vocabulary

A Find the words in the box in Reading 2. Use the context and the words in parentheses to help you choose the correct word to complete each of the following sentences.

| occurrence (Par. 1) | location (Par. 3) | monitor (Par. 7) |
| habitats (Par. 1) | despite (Par. 4) | limit (Par. 7) |

1. Scientists are concerned that the natural _____ (environments where an animal lives) of the tiger are disappearing as cities expand into the Indian forests.

2. The doctors carefully _____ (pay attention to) their patients to make sure that the children recover quickly.

3. There are now so many alligators in Miami that it is quite a common _____ (event or incident) to see one right in the city area.

4. Many wildlife experts argue that the government should _____ (control) the number of hunters who are legally allowed to shoot wild animals.

5. The vet was able to rescue the injured elephant _____ (even though there was) the danger from the other elephants in the herd.

6. We didn't know the exact _____ (particular place) of the school, but we used our cell phones and quickly found it.

B The academic words in bold often appear with the words on the right. Complete the paragraph by choosing the correct word on the right to combine with each academic word.

a(n) _____ **occurrence**   common, unusual

a(n) _____ **location**   exact, quiet

(to) **limit** _____   the number of, the price of

despite _____   the fact that, the hard work

_____ **habitat**   natural, urban

_____ **monitoring**   closely, rarely

In the forests of the Pacific Northwest, an area of the United States, scientists are _____

monitoring the _____ habitat of the
                           2
Spotted Owl. They are trying to find the

_____ location of where the birds
              3
nest. Yet these birds are now so rare that seeing one is

a very _____ occurrence. These
                  4
owls need trees for shelter and hunting. Scientists have

been able to limit _____ of
                              5
companies that are cutting trees in this area. However,

despite _____ of the scientists, this owl is
                        6
still in great danger.

Multiword Vocabulary

A Find the multiword vocabulary in bold in Reading 2. Use the context to help you understand the meaning. Then match each item to the correct definition.

_____ **1. all kinds of** (Par. 1)

_____ **2. at an alarming rate** (Par. 2)

_____ **3. arrives at the scene** (Par. 4)

_____ **4. foster care** (Par. 6)

_____ **5. go about** (Par. 7)

_____ **6. is at stake** (Par. 7)

a. be the way you approach a task

b. looking after someone else's children for a short time

c. a great variety of

d. very quickly

e. gets to where something is happening

f. is at risk

B Complete the following sentences with the correct multiword vocabulary from Exercise A.

1. Peter was an experienced volunteer, so he knew exactly how to

   _____ rescuing the homeless dogs.

2. The World Wildlife Organization warns that nations must do more to protect the tiger because the future of this animal _____.

3. The zoo's vet often travels many miles to rescue animals. When she

   _____, she has to figure out the safest way to help the injured animal.

4. In many urban areas in the United States, the number of coyotes is increasing

   _____. People are worried because this animal hunts pets such as cats.

5. The boy lived in _____ for a number of years because his parents were not able to take care of him.

6. The children always enjoy going to the pet store because there are

   _____ animals, fish, and reptiles.

Use the Vocabulary

Write answers to the following questions. Use the words in bold in your answers. Then share your answers with a partner.

1. How does technology help us to quickly figure out the **exact location** of a place?

2. Teachers often say that we should **limit the number of** young children in a class to around 20. Is this a good idea? Do you think children learn more effectively in small classes?

3. What **is at stake** if we do not conserve water? What might happen in the future?

4. In some parts of the world, people are cutting down forests **at an alarming rate**. Why are they doing this? What are some of the results of losing this **natural habitat**?

5. Experts are worried because the number of tigers is falling very quickly in India. What can the Indian government do to **closely monitor** the safety of these animals?

6. One day, you are walking to school and you see a car accident. You rush over to help, and you are the first to **arrive at the scene**. One car is on fire. What do you do?

THINK AND DISCUSS

Work in a small group. Use the information in the reading and your own ideas to discuss the following questions.

1. **Summarize.** Why are koalas in danger?

2. **Evaluate the author's opinion.** De Villiers believes that the government should pass laws to limit new construction in koala habitat. Do you think this is a good way to protect animals?

3. **Identify solutions.** What are some other ways Australians can protect koalas?

Krithi Karanth

Vocabulary Review

A Complete the paragraphs with the vocabulary below that you have studied in the unit.

are at stake	common occurrence	expanding into	natural habitat
closely monitoring	despite the hard work	go about	rapid urbanization

Can one billion people, tigers, and elephants live together peacefully in India? Indian biologist Krithi Karanth believes they must. This is because the lives of both people and animals

_____ . Yet there are challenges. India is experiencing strong economic
              1

growth and _____ . This is reducing the _____ of
              2   3

wildlife. Farms, villages, and cities are _____ the forests. Coming face-to-face
                                          4

with wild animals is a _____ . In addition, illegal hunting is growing,
                        5

_____ of conservation organizations to control it.
6

Karanth and her colleagues in India believe that they might know how to

_____ fixing this problem. They are _____ both human
7   8

and animal populations. They are working with the Indian government to find solutions to human-wildlife problems. In addition, they are educating communities about how to protect their farms from wild animals. Karanth hopes their efforts will make a difference and improve the lives of humans and wildlife. This needs to happen soon, however. Tigers, elephants, and other species are fast disappearing.

B Compare answers to Exercise A with a partner. Then discuss the following questions.

Why does Karanth believe one billion people and wildlife can live together? Do you think that wild tigers will only be a memory in the future?

C Complete the following sentences in a way that shows that you understand the meaning of the words in bold.

1. When I moved to another country, it was difficult to get used to the very hot weather. My parents found it difficult **to get used to** _____.

2. Governments should provide **foster care** because _____.

3. Getting a passport is a complicated **process**. Another complicated process is _____.

4. At work, it is important to know how to **interact with** others because _____.

D Work with a partner and write four sentences that include any four of the vocabulary items below. You may use any verb tense and make nouns plural if you want.

all kinds of	exact location	step-by-step
arrive at the scene	leave behind	take turns

Connect the Readings

A Look back at Readings 1 and 2 to complete the chart below. Put a check (✓) in the boxes to show which topics appeared in each reading. Note that some topics appeared in both readings.

	Reading 1	Reading 2
1. Effects of urbanization		
2. The importance of volunteers		
3. Human-animal interaction		
4. Wild animals cause damage		
5. Illegal hunting		
6. Plans to save wildlife		
7. Wildlife experts		
8. Working long hours to save animals		

B Compare your chart with a partner. Then quickly scan the readings in order to find some specific details that support each topic.

C Discuss the following questions with a partner. Use your understanding of the readings and your own ideas.

1. Look at the eight topics in the chart above. Which three of these topics do you think are the most important?

2. Which topic is the most interesting to you? Why?

3. When an animal species is in danger of disappearing, we call it *endangered*. What species other than the elephant and the koala are endangered in the world today? What do you think will happen to these animals in the future?

VOLCANIC ISLANDS

Tourists holding flashlights
watch the Kilauea volcano
erupt in Hawaii, USA.

1. What are some of the well-known islands in the world?

2. Have you ever visited an island? Have you ever lived on one?

3. How do you think some islands are formed?

147

Academic Vocabulary

| additional | to measure | privileged |
| to contribute | multiple | revenue |

Multiword Vocabulary

to be anything but	in spite of
for the time being	nothing out of the ordinary
history repeats itself	to see something up close

Iceland and Hawaii are very different places—but not in every way. Read on to learn what these amazing islands have in common.

Reading Preview

A **Preview.** Work in a small group. Read the title and the first sentence of each paragraph on pages 150–151. Look at the photos. Then discuss the following questions with a partner or in a small group.

1. The title refers to the tall, young, and active. What are these words describing?

2. The photos are of islands in different parts of the world. What do they have in common with each other?

3. What dangers do some of these islands face?

B **Topic vocabulary.** The following words appear in Reading 1. Look at the words and answer the questions with a partner.

active	frequent	smoke
eruptions	island	underwater
exciting	ocean	violent
explode		

1. Which words might describe volcanoes?

2. Which words relate to water?

3. Which words are connected with danger?

C **Predict.** What do you think this reading will be about? Discuss each word in Exercise B and predict how it may relate to the reading.

Steam rises from Mount Gharat on the volcanic island of Gaua in the South Pacific Ocean.

Tall, Young, and Active

TALL, YOUNG, AND ACTIVE

November 14, 1963, was a cold morning. 1
This was nothing out of the ordinary
for the fishermen. They were used to
the winter weather around Iceland. Suddenly,
however, they saw something unusual. Thick,
black smoke was pouring out of the sea. Thinking
a boat was on fire, they raced toward it. Yet, as
they got closer, they realized it was something
quite different. Magma[1] was erupting from the
ocean floor. The fishermen watched as a new
island rose from the sea. Later named Surtsey,
this island joined the thousands of volcanic
islands worldwide.

The island of Hawaii is one of the most 2
well-known volcanic islands. Lava from multiple
volcanoes built this island. One of these
volcanoes is Mauna Kea. Mauna Kea began under
the ocean over a million years ago. Magma broke
through the Earth's crust—that is, the outer layer
of the Earth. As the magma cooled, it formed an
underwater mountain. About 800,000 years ago,

the mountain rose above sea level. Eruptions then
became more frequent and more violent. Layers
of lava (magma that pours out of the volcano)
hardened into rock. Now, Mauna Kea measures
9,966 meters from ocean floor to mountain peak.
This makes it the world's highest mountain.

Fortunately for Hawaiians, Mauna Kea 3
volcano is quiet—for the time being. Another
volcano on the same island is anything but quiet.
Kilauea is smaller than Mauna Kea. However, it
has erupted nonstop since 1983. It is the world's
most active volcano. Every day, it produces
between 300,000 and 600,000 square meters of
lava. Over the past two decades, it has added
more than 540 acres (218 hectares) to the island.
In spite of the danger, it is a popular tourist
attraction. As a popular tourist attraction, it also
contributes millions of dollars to the Hawaiian
economy. Yet this revenue and additional land
have come at a cost. Kilauea is responsible for
taking both lives and homes.

Mauna Kea is the world's tallest mountain. 4
Kilauea is the world's most active volcano.

---

[1] *magma:* very hot, melted rock below the Earth's surface

Kilauea lava flow near Kalapana, Hawaii, USA

Until recently, Surtsey was the youngest island. Then, on December 19, 2011, history repeated itself. Fishermen were again privileged to see the birth of a new island up close. Smoke and red-hot magma exploded from the sea. This time, however, the fishermen were from Yemen. They were on a boat in the warm waters of the Red Sea. A few days later, a small island appeared. This became one of the world's newest volcanic islands.

READING COMPREHENSION

Big Picture

A Read the following statements. Check (✓) the four statements that express the main ideas of Reading 1.

_____ **1.** Icelandic fishermen saw the beginning of Surtsey in 1963.

_____ **2.** One of the world's newest islands is off the coast of Yemen.

_____ **3.** Mauna Kea rose above sea level 800,000 years ago.

_____ **4.** Kilauea, on the island of Hawaii, is the world's most active volcano.

_____ **5.** Kilauea is very dangerous because it is constantly erupting.

_____ **6.** Many islands are formed by underwater volcanoes.

_____ **7.** The volcano Mauna Kea is the world's highest mountain.

B Compare answers to Exercise A with a partner. Then complete the following activity.

1. Reread your four main ideas. Scan Reading 1 to find the order in which they appear. Write the main ideas on the blank lines in the correct order.

   a. _____

   b. _____

   c. _____

   d. _____

2. Which of these main ideas is the main idea of the *whole* reading? _____

Close-Up

Choose the word or phrase that best completes each of the following sentences.

1. The men fishing off the coast of Iceland thought the smoke was coming from a _____.
   a. boat   **b.** volcano

2. _____ volcanoes were responsible for forming the island of Hawaii.
   a. Two   **b.** Many

3. After Mauna Kea rose above sea level, it erupted _____ frequently.
   a. more   **b.** less

4. If you measure Mauna Kea from _____ to its highest point, it is the world's highest mountain.
   a. sea level   **b.** ocean floor

5. Mauna Kea _____ active right now.
   a. is not   **b.** is

6. The island of Hawaii is growing in size because of _____.
   a. Mauna Kea   **b.** Kilauea

7. In December 2011, history repeated itself when fishermen saw the birth of another island _____ part of the world _____ Surtsey.

   a. in the same . . . as   **b.** in a different . . . from

8. Surtsey and the island off the coast of Yemen are examples of very _____ volcanic islands.

   a. new   **b.** old

Reading Skill

Understanding and Learning Technical Terms

In Unit 4 (page 81), you learned that writers often help students understand the meaning of important vocabulary. Writers also help students understand technical terms— vocabulary that is specific to a subject. Each subject has its own technical terms. Good readers make sure they understand and remember these terms.

Example

Although it has not erupted in years, Mount Rainer in the United States is an active volcano (a volcano that has erupted in the past 10,000 years is called active).

These strategies will help you to understand technical terms:

- Look for glossed words. A glossed word is almost always important. Check the meaning at the bottom of the page.
- Check for definition signals such as *that is* and *or*. A definition may follow.
- Check for definition punctuation such as a dash or parentheses.

To remember technical terms:

- Read the words around the terms. See how the writer uses the term in a sentence.
- Write the word on one side of a note card. Write the definition on the other side.
- When you have several cards, test yourself. Read the key term out loud. Explain its meaning. Check the back of the card to see if you have defined it correctly.

A Reread Reading 1. Make a list of technical terms. Then find their definitions and compete the following chart.

Technical Terms	Definitions

B Compare your definitions with a partner. Then make note cards for each term. Test yourself and your partner. Change the order of the cards as you do this.

VOCABULARY PRACTICE

Academic Vocabulary

A Find the words in bold in Reading 1. Use their context to help you match each word to the definition.

_____ **1. multiple** (Par. 2)

_____ **2. measures** (Par. 2)

_____ **3. contributes** (Par. 3)

_____ **4. revenue** (Par. 3)

_____ **5. additional** (Par. 3)

_____ **6. privileged** (Par. 4)

a. fortunate

b. money that governments or businesses earn

c. is a certain height or size

d. gives money or ideas to help someone

e. many

f. more, extra

B Work with a partner to choose a word from the box to complete each of the following sentences. The words in bold often appear with the academic words in the box.

additional	contributes	measures	multiple	privileged	revenue

1. The newspaper reporter decided he needed _____ **information** before he could publish his story. He was missing some key facts about the accident.

2. Jane's business is doing very well. As a result, she announced that because of **increased** _____ from sales, she was going to hire ten more employees.

3. Hiro was a very nervous driver. He took his driver's test _____ **times** before he passed.

4. The tallest tree in the park _____ 363 **feet** in height.

5. Susan is a valuable employee because she always _____ good **ideas** at company meetings.

6. I **feel** _____ to be attending this university. The classes are excellent, and the professors are very helpful.

Multiword Vocabulary

A Find each multiword vocabulary in bold in Reading 1. Use the context to help you understand the meaning. Then match each item to its definition.

_____ **1. nothing out of the ordinary** (Par. 1)

_____ **2. for the time being** (Par. 3)

_____ **3. is anything but** (Par. 3)

_____ **4. in spite of** (Par. 3)

_____ **5. history repeated itself** (Par. 4)

_____ **6. see** (something) **up close** (Par. 4)

a. not affected by some bad condition

b. have a good view

c. is the opposite of

d. normal

e. for right now

f. the same events happened over and over again

B Complete the following sentences with the correct multiword vocabulary from Exercise A.

1. _____ the heat, the photographer was able to get close to the lava and take some amazing pictures.

2. Smoke was coming from the volcano, but this was _____ because there had been smoke for weeks. Suddenly, however, the whole mountain exploded.

3. World War I was called the war to end all wars. However, 21 years later, _____ and World War II started.

4. The firefighters announced that the fire was out _____. However, they warned that lightning could start another fire at any time.

5. The tourists went up in a helicopter over Kilauea. Although it was expensive, they said it was amazing to _____ this volcano _____.

6. Sometimes the Web _____ helpful. It has so much information that it can be very confusing.

Use the Vocabulary

Write answers to the following questions. Use the words in bold in your answers. Then share your answers with a partner.

1. Most schools provide **multiple** opportunities for students to improve their English. What are some of the opportunities at your school? Are you using them?

2. Do you need **additional** help in any of your classes? What kind of help is available?

3. Feeling nervous before a test **is nothing out of the ordinary**. What do you do to help yourself calm down before a test begins?

4. Some very large companies **contribute** a lot of money to schools. Can you think of a company that does this? How is helping schools good for business?

5. Reading 1 talked about a volcanologist who takes risks in order to **see** volcanoes **up close**. Can you think of other scientists who face danger in order to do their work?

6. The expression *history repeats itself* suggests that humans do not learn from their mistakes. Do you agree with this? Can you think of some examples?

7. What is something you have been successful at **in spite of** the difficulties you faced?

THINK AND DISCUSS

Work in a small group. Use the information in the reading and your own ideas to discuss the following questions.

1. **Analyze.** "Kilauea has been both good and bad for the island of Hawaii." What does this statement mean?

2. **Relate to personal knowledge.** People live in areas near volcanoes in spite of the danger. Why do you think they do this?

3. **Express an opinion.** Would you like to see an active volcano up close? Explain your answer.

A view of a low-lying island in the Maldives—a group of islands in the Indian Ocean

Academic Vocabulary

a debate	obvious	to relax
gradually	overseas	to relocate

Multiword Vocabulary

the beauty of something	to draw attention to (something)
to be made up of	no matter how
to be well aware of	of even greater concern

Reading Preview

A **Preview.** Scan Reading 2 for definitions of the following terms. Write the definitions on the lines. Then compare your answers with a partner or in a small group.

coral: _____

artificial islands: _____

atoll: _____

B **Topic vocabulary.** The following words appear in Reading 2. Look at the words and answer the questions with a partner.

beaches	islands	sinking
diving	luxury	sunbathe
golf	resorts	threat
hotel		

1. Which words are places tourists visit?
2. Which words are about activities and things tourists might enjoy?
3. Which words are connected to problems?

C **Predict.** What do you think this reading will be about? Discuss each word in Exercise B and predict how it may relate to the reading.

Imagine you live on a tropical island, but your home is disappearing into the sea. Read about a place where this is happening right now.

An Uncertain Future

W elcome to the island nation of the Maldives. Palm trees, miles of white sand beaches, and warm, calm waters are waiting for you. Come to relax in a luxury hotel and sunbathe by the pool. Come to play golf. Or come to dive and marvel[1] at the thousands of marine species in these crystal clear waters. But come fairly soon, for this tropical paradise is sinking.

The Maldives is made up of 1,190 islands in the Indian Ocean. The average height of each island is just 5 feet (1.5 meters) above sea level. And the sea level is rising. In the last century, it has risen 7 inches (17.8 centimeters). Of even greater concern, in the last decade sea levels have been rising more quickly than before. This is bad news for the people of this nation. It is also not good for the thousands of tourists who plan to visit this country sometime in the future.

An obvious question comes to mind: Why are these islands so low? The answer lies in their formation. First, each island begins with underwater volcanic eruptions. As a result of these eruptions, underwater mountains slowly rise above the water. Then coral[2] begins to grow

in the water around the edge of these islands. Then, over millions of years the middle of the island slowly sinks back into the sea, but the coral continues to grow. As waves break apart some of this coral, it turns into white sand. Finally, a sandy area gradually becomes a ring-shaped island, or atoll. All the time, waves and ocean currents are moving the sand around. This prevents sand from piling up, and it prevents the atoll from growing higher than a few feet.

Changing sea levels can easily damage the low-lying atolls. Sea levels are rising because of climate change. The Maldivians are well aware of this threat. In 2009, then president Mohammed Nasheed explained, "We no longer have the luxury of debate. For us, climate change is real. We are already relocating people from 16 islands affected by rising seas to other areas of our country." Nasheed thought of an effective way to draw attention to the problem. He and his top officials put on diving gear and held the world's first underwater government meeting.

The Maldivians cannot stop the rising seas. So their government is making plans to move more people, perhaps even to different countries. They have also come up with a very innovative idea to save their country—artificial, or man-made, islands. The government is working with a Dutch company to explore the idea of building

---

[1] *marvel:* be very surprised at how beautiful something is
[2] *coral:* a collection of very small, hard creatures that grow in warm seawater

One of the floating islands of Uros, Peru

ARTIFICIAL ISLANDS

Artificial islands are not a new idea. Centuries ago, the Uros people of Peru were fighting the more powerful Incas. To protect themselves, they built floating islands out of grass. Today, about 300 Uros people still live on these islands. More recently, several countries have created artificial islands. Japan, the Netherlands, and the United Arab Emirates, for example, have all built islands for airports or housing.

Members of the Maldavian government meet underwater. They want world governments to work together to stop rising sea levels.

One of the Maldive Islands

these islands. If the government goes ahead with this project, the company will build the new islands overseas. Ships will then take them to the Maldives. Once in place, huge chains will anchor[3] these islands to the ocean floor.

Each of the man-made islands will have a   6 different design and purpose. Some islands will have very expensive houses. Others will have luxury resorts. One island will be a golf course. Underwater tunnels will connect other islands to this golf course. There will also be islands with affordable housing for residents. And the beauty of this plan? The artificial islands will float above the water level, no matter how high the sea rises in the future.

---

[3] *anchor:* make to stay in one place in the water with a heavy hooked object

READING COMPREHENSION

Big Picture

A Choose the sentence that best completes each of the following sentences.

1. What is the main idea of paragraph 2?
   a. The Maldives is made up of over 1,000 islands.
   b. Rising sea levels are a threat to these low islands.
   c. The sea level has risen more than five inches in the past 100 years.
   d. Thousands of tourists plan to visit the Maldives.

2. What is the main idea of paragraph 3?
   a. The Maldives are extremely low.
   b. It takes millions of years for these islands to form.
   c. Wind and ocean currents prevent sand from piling up.
   d. Atolls are naturally low-lying because of the way they are formed.

3. What is the main idea of paragraph 4?
   a. Climate change is a real threat in the Maldives.
   b. Former President Nasheed drew attention to the problem of rising sea levels.
   c. Nasheed moved people from the lowest islands.
   d. The Maldives faces a serious problem because of sinking coral.

4. What is the main idea of paragraph 5?
   a. Man-made islands are one creative way to save the Maldives.
   b. A Dutch company is designing several different types of islands.
   c. The Maldivian government is coming up with innovative solutions.
   d. The Dutch company will transport the islands to the Maldives.

5. What is the main idea of paragraph 6?
   a. Some islands will have luxury hotels.
   b. Tourists will be able to play golf on these islands.
   c. People will be able to reach islands by an underwater tunnel.
   d. The islands are designed for different purposes.

B Read the following statements. Check (✓) the statement that expresses the main idea of the *whole* reading.

_____ 1. Climate change is responsible for rising sea levels.

_____ 2. The Maldives Islands are examples of low-lying atolls.

_____ 3. Maldivians are thinking of ways to save their sinking islands.

_____ 4. The Maldivian government has already moved some people to higher ground.

Close-Up

(A) Decide which of the following statements are true or false according to Reading 2 and the short extra reading, "Artificial Islands," on page 158. Write *T* (True) or *F* (False) next to each one.

_____ **1.** In the last century, the sea level has risen five feet above the Maldives.

_____ **2.** The Maldives is made up of volcanic islands.

_____ **3.** Over millions of years, the middle of an atoll constantly grows.

_____ **4.** Only the wind stops the atoll from getting higher than a few meters.

_____ **5.** President Nasheed explained why he could not move any Maldivians to a safer place.

_____ **6.** Nasheed was very concerned about the threat of climate change.

_____ **7.** Nasheed believed that countries should spend more time discussing the problems before they take action.

_____ **8.** The Dutch company will build the artificial islands in a different country and tow them to the Maldives.

_____ **9.** Rising sea levels will not affect artificial islands.

_____ **10.** The Maldives is the first country ever to consider the use of man-made islands.

(B) Work with a partner or in a small group. Change the false statements in Exercise A to make them true.

Reading Skill

Understanding a Process

Academic textbooks often explain a process, or how something happens. This is particularly common in courses such as biology, geography, and geology. Writers divide a process into a series of steps. This makes it easier to understand.

Read this example from Reading 2:

An obvious question comes to mind: Why are these islands so low? The answer lies in their formation. First, each island begins with underwater volcanic eruptions. As a result of these eruptions, underwater mountains slowly rise above the water. Then coral begins to grow . . .

Note that this process paragraph begins with a question. Then it starts to answer that question. It begins with the first of a series of steps. It goes on to explain these steps in order.

To make a process clear, writers use:

- Signal words (*first, next, begins, then, finally*) to introduce and connect a series of steps.
- Definitions of important terms.

A Read the following process paragraph. Then complete the activities that follow.

It is hard to imagine that the beautiful islands of Hawaii began as islands of brown rock. How do volcanic islands change into these green islands full of life? This process begins when the volcanic island first rises above sea level. Then, the wind and the rain start to break down some of the rock into soil. This is known as erosion. Next, the wind and the rain carry seeds that fall onto this soil. The wind can even carry small creatures such as spiders. At the same time, birds fly to the new island, carrying more seeds and insects. Marine animals such as crabs arrive on the waves. Then larger animals are carried across on floating islands made of trash and pieces of wood. Finally, people arrive and bring more animals and plants. This change from brown rock to green islands is called colonization.

1. What question does this paragraph answer?

_____

2. What is this process called?

_____

3. What three terms are explained in this paragraph?

_____

4. Reread the paragraph. As you read, number each part of the process.

5. Which signal words does the writer use to help you understand the different steps? Write them here:

_____

B The following sentences explain how atolls form. Use information from Reading 2, paragraph 3 to number the sentences in the correct order. Then compare your answers with a partner.

_____ The center of the island very slowly sinks back into the sea.

_____ The coral reef slowly changes into an island in the shape of a ring.

_____ An underwater volcano erupts and begins to form a mountain.

_____ As the center sinks, coral continues to grow.

_____ This type of island is called an atoll.

_____ The volcanic mountain slowly rises above sea level.

_____ Coral begins to grow around the outside edges of the rising mountain.

VOCABULARY PRACTICE

Academic Vocabulary

A Find the words in the box in Reading 2. Use the context and the words in parentheses to help you choose the correct word to complete each of the following sentences.

relax (Par. 1)	gradually (Par. 3)	relocating (Par. 4)
obvious (Par. 3)	debate (Par. 4)	overseas (Par. 5)

1. There is a(n) _____ (clear) reason why thousands of people visit Hawaii each year: The islands are beautiful.

2. The storm has destroyed many houses near the ocean, and the government is busy _____ (moving) over a hundred families to higher ground.

3. There is still a heated _____ (discussion) about the causes of climate change.

4. As the temperature rose, the thick ice _____ (slowly) melted and turned into water.

5. The company closed its factories in France and moved all its business _____ (to another country).

6. The government said it would not _____ (make less strict) the laws about building houses close to the water. It is worried that if it does, more people will build homes on the beaches, and this is harmful to the environment.

B Read the following sentences and choose the correct word or phrase to complete each one. Write the word or phrase on the line.

1. I was very lucky to have the opportunity to _____ **overseas**.
   a. read about   **b.** study

2. There is a _____ **debate** about how to improve the teaching of math in schools.
   a. fierce   **b.** happy

3. The child had been very sick, but he was **gradually** _____.
   a. still very weak   **b.** getting better

4. On the island of Hawaii, the government **relocated** some _____ because they were too close to Kilauea.

    a. people   **b.** times

5. Students asked permission to use dictionaries on a test, but the teacher refused to **relax** her very strict _____ .

    a. vacation   **b.** rules

6. For **obvious** _____ , when you vote it must be secret; no one can know who you voted for.

    a. reasons   **b.** explanations

Multiword Vocabulary

(A) Find the multiword vocabulary in bold in Reading 2. Use the context to help you understand the meaning. Then match each item to the correct definition.

_____ **1. is made up of** (Par. 2)	**a.** clearly realize or know what is happening
_____ **2. of even greater concern** (Par. 2)	**b.** the best thing about
_____ **3. are well aware of** (Par. 4)	**c.** consists of, contains
_____ **4. draw attention to** (Par. 4)	**d.** something is true or happens whatever the situation
_____ **5. the beauty of** (Par. 6)	**e.** even more worrying
_____ **6. no matter how** (Par. 6)	**f.** make others think about

(B) Complete the following paragraph with the correct multiword vocabulary from Exercise A.

Many hotels in the Maldives are in danger of flooding from heavy rain. _____ is flooding from rising sea levels. So hotel managers are
                1
trying to improve safety. They know that all hotel employees _____
                                                 2
the danger of floods, but they also know employees are busy and sometimes forget what to do in an
emergency. So the managers decided to _____ the danger by
                                                          3
making colorful posters. These posters explain what to do if there is a flood. _____ these posters is that they are so simple, even young children
                    4
can understand them. In addition to the posters, each hotel will have safety kits for all its residents.
Each kit _____ emergency food, clean water, and a blanket.
                                      5
_____ bad the flood, everyone who works for a hotel must be able
                6
to help tourists. After all, it is the responsibility of all employees to keep the tourists safe.

The man-made Palm Jumeirah Island off Dubai in the United Arab Emirates

Use the Vocabulary

Write answers to the following questions. Use the words in bold in your answers. Then share your answers with a partner.

1. What do you do to **relax**—particularly in stressful times?

2. What natural dangers are there in your area? How does the government try to **draw attention to** these problems and educate residents?

3. What are some reasons why people **relocate** to a different area?

4. Why do many companies move their business **overseas**?

5. Many high school students worry about getting good grades. **Of even greater concern**, however, is getting into a university. Why do so many students worry about getting into a good university?

6. In an American college or university, many students do not choose their major until the second or third year. They take general courses for the first two years. **The beauty of this** is that students can explore different courses and subjects. Do you agree this is a good thing? Or do you think it is better to start studying your major as soon as you enter the school?

7. Students often feel frustrated because it takes a long time to learn a language. Is your English **gradually** improving? In what area are you making the most progress?

THINK AND DISCUSS

Work in a small group. Use the information in the reading and your own ideas to discuss the following questions.

1. **Summarize.** What problems are facing the people of Hawaii and the people of the Maldives?

2. **Express an opinion.** Should the governments pay to relocate people if their homes are in danger due to a natural problem such as volcanoes or rising seas? Or should people be responsible for moving themselves?

3. **Evaluate.** Why is building artificial islands an ambitious project? Do you think the Maldives will go ahead with this plan? Explain your answer.

Vocabulary Review

A Complete the paragraph with the vocabulary below that you have studied in the unit.

for the time being	in spite of	nothing out of the ordinary	relocate people
history repeated itself	multiple times	obvious reasons	was anything but

The morning of August 27, 1883, began as normal on the Indonesian island of Krakatoa. Smoke and ash rose from the volcano. This latest eruption was _____ because Krakatoa had erupted _____ since May of that year. However, by 10:00 a.m. the situation _____ normal. There was suddenly a huge explosion that threw rock and dust 24 miles into the air. The sound was enormous. People as far away as Australia heard it. In a period of 19 hours, the island destroyed itself and 30,000 people died.

Then in 1927, _____. Fishermen saw smoke and ash over the old Krakatoa. A few days later, another volcano rose out of the sea. Indonesians call this Anak, or child of, Krakatoa. Like its parent, this volcano is also very active. The Indonesian government is well aware of the danger. The population in this area is much larger today than it was 130 years ago. Also, _____ the danger, Anak Krakatoa has become a tourist attraction. For _____, the government worries that the volcano will erupt again. They also worry about the possibility of a tsunami—that is, a huge wave caused by a volcanic eruption. Government leaders are trying to _____ to a safer area, but many residents do not want to leave their homes. _____, the Child of Krakatoa is quite well behaved, but we don't know how it will behave in the future.

B Compare answers to Exercise A with a partner. Then discuss the following questions.

"The Indonesian government is worried that history may repeat itself." What does this statement mean? Do you think the government is right to be worried?

C Complete the following sentences in a way that shows you understand the meaning of the words in bold.

1. I think teachers should **relax their rules** about _____.

2. _____ is **gradually getting better** because _____.

3. In my country, people argue about smoking in public places. There is also a **fierce debate** about

   _____.

4. I couldn't finish my essay because I needed **additional information**, so I _____.

D Work with a partner and write four sentences that include any four of the vocabulary items below. You may use any verb tense and make nouns plural if you want.

be made up of	draw attention to	increased revenue
be well aware of	feel privileged	studying overseas

Connect the Readings

A Use information from Readings 1 and 2 to complete the exercises.

1. Label the illustration, using the correct technical vocabulary.

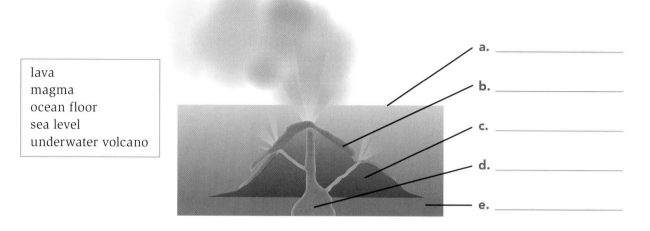

lava
magma
ocean floor
sea level
underwater volcano

a. _____

b. _____

c. _____

d. _____

e. _____

2. Complete the chart below.

	Reading 1	Reading 2
a. What new technical vocabulary did you learn from each reading?		
b. How are the islands of Hawaii (Reading 1) similar to the islands of the Maldives (Reading 2)?		
c. How are the two groups of islands in each reading different?		
d. What was the most surprising fact you learned from each reading?		

B With a partner or in a small group, compare answers to Exercise A. Then discuss the following question.

Why is life on volcanic islands sometimes difficult or dangerous?

C Discuss the following questions with a partner. Use your understanding of the readings and your own ideas.

1. This unit describes several famous volcanic eruptions. What other eruptions have you heard about? If necessary, go online for information. Describe what happened.

2. Have you ever heard of a tsunami? Where and when did one take place? What happened?

3. Some people think that tsunamis are of greater concern than volcanoes. Do you agree?

People move giant pieces during a game of Chinese chess in Zhoushan, China. The best Chinese chess players can remember moves, ideas, and patterns from thousands of games.

FOCUS
1. Do you think you have a good or bad memory? Give examples.
2. What do you do to help you remember important information, such as for a test?

MEMORY

Academic Vocabulary

to conclude	findings	stressful
a factor	physically	unique

Multiword Vocabulary

to beat oneself up	to not be the case
every single	on the other hand
to give someone a break	to shed light on

Reading Preview

(A) Preview. Read the title and the first sentence of each paragraph on pages 172–173. Then discuss the following questions with a partner or in a small group.

1. How good is your memory? What were you doing two Saturdays ago at 4:00 p.m.? How much can you remember?

2. Who is AJ? Why are researchers studying her?

3. What are some advantages of having a really good memory?

(B) Topic vocabulary. The following words appear in Reading 1. Look at the words and answer the questions with a partner.

ability	gift
autobiographical	memory
average	nerve
brain	recall
exceptional	uncontrollable

1. What is a "brain"? Which words are related to the brain?

2. Which adjectives describe memory?

3. The word *gift* has two meanings. One meaning is "a present" and the other is "a natural ability." What do some people have a gift for?

(C) Predict. What do you think this reading will be about? Discuss each word in Exercise B and predict how it may relate to the reading.

How well do you remember events from your past? Most of us remember a few important days in our lives. But what if you could remember every detail of every day? Meet someone who can!

Asian elephant in Elephant Nature Park, Chiang Mai Thailand. Both elephants and humans are mammals with excellent memories.

An Amazing Memory

The majority of us can remember what we were doing last Saturday at 4:00 p.m. If we think for a minute, we can probably recall the Saturday before that. In contrast, go back a few months, and most of us will have trouble remembering. We usually can't remember what we were doing at a specific time on a specific day. Those of us with average memories simply forget these details. And this is normal. We remember what we need and what we think is important. The rest, we forget.

This is not the case, however, for a few people with extraordinary[1] memories. AJ from California is one of these people. She remembers every single detail of last Saturday, and the Saturday before that. In fact, she remembers every detail of almost every day of her life since age 11. She remembers that at 12:34 p.m. on Sunday, August 3, 1986, a young man called her on the telephone. What was she doing at noon, March 28, 1992? She was having lunch with her father in the Beverly Hills Hotel. "My memory flows like a movie— nonstop and uncontrollable," she explains.

_____
[1] *extraordinary:* not average; very unusual

AJ was in seventh grade when she first realized that her memory was unusual. "I was not happy because I hated school. I started thinking about the year before. . . . But then I started realizing that I was remembering the exact date and exactly what I was doing a year ago that day." At this point, she knew her memory was exceptional. As she grew older, her unique ability continued to develop. Today, she might have one of the best memories in the world.

Researchers have studied AJ for many years. They are coming up with some interesting findings. AJ can recall personal events on any day in the last 35 years. On the other hand, researchers found that she doesn't score very well on standard memory tests. She has difficulty remembering a series of numbers, for example. So her amazing memory only relates to her own life. For this reason, scientists call her memory autobiographical. Only a handful of people worldwide have this type of memory.

These people have two interesting things in common. First, parts of their brains are physically different from the brain of a person with average memory. For example, the nerve

A woman holds a photo of herself as a child.

connections between the middle and front of the brain are stronger. Equally important, people like AJ can't stop thinking about the past. They keep diaries. They read old newspapers. In other words, they work hard to remember the past. These two factors are beginning to shed light on autobiographical memory.

Remembering everything has its advantages. Yet it can also be very stressful. "I remember good [things], which is very comforting. But I also remember bad [things]—and every bad choice," AJ explains. "And I don't give myself a break . . . I am still beating myself up over them." She concludes, "Most people have called what I have a gift, but I call it a burden.[2]"

6

_____

[2] *burden:* a problem that causes a person a lot of difficulty and worry

READING COMPREHENSION

Big Picture

A Read the following statements. Check (✓) the six statements that express the main ideas of Reading 1.

_____ **1.** AJ discovered her unique ability when she was a child.

_____ **2.** An amazing memory can be very stressful.

_____ **3.** AJ can remember every day of her first week at school.

_____ **4.** At school, AJ was not good at taking tests.

_____ **5.** The average person forgets most details in his or her life.

_____ **6.** Two factors explain autobiographical memory.

_____ **7.** Researchers have found that memory changes as you get older.

_____ **8.** AJ has an extraordinary memory.

_____ **9.** Autobiographical memory is a specific type of memory.

_____ **10.** AJ has had a happy life.

B Compare answers to Exercise A with a partner. Then put the main ideas in the order in which they appear in Reading 1.

1. _____   **2.** _____   **3.** _____   **4.** _____   **5.** _____   **6.** _____

Close-Up

A Choose the word or phrase that best completes each of the following sentences.

1. It is very _____ for the typical person to forget the majority of specific details that happen in his or her life.

   a. normal   **b.** unusual

2. AJ realized her ability to remember was very unusual when she _____.

   a. began school   **b.** was in seventh grade

3. School was a particularly _____ time for AJ.

   a. happy   **b.** challenging

4. AJ is _____ who have the ability to remember autobiographical details in such detail.

    a. like many others   **b.** one of a few people

5. AJ can easily recall her own life, _____ numerical information such as long telephone numbers.

    a. but not   **b.** as well as

6. People with autobiographical memories have _____ connections between the nerves in the middle and front of their brains.

    a. better   **b.** weaker

7. Although she has an extraordinary memory, AJ _____ to improve her ability to remember specific events.

    a. continues   **b.** doesn't try

8. Scientists explain that autobiographical memory is _____ the result of physical factors such as differences in brains.

    a. completely   **b.** only partly

9. AJ tends to think _____ about mistakes she has made in the past.

    a. a little   **b.** a lot

10. AJ believes that, overall, her extraordinary memory has been _____ for her.

    a. good   **b.** difficult

B Compare answers to Exercise A with a partner. If you have different answers, go back and check the reading.

Reading Skill

Connecting Personal Experiences to a Reading

Academic reading often includes information about the lives of other people. Good readers connect their own experiences and opinions with this type of reading. This personal connection helps them more fully understand the person they are reading about.

Readers connect to a reading by asking questions as they read. Questions will vary according to what they are reading. Some examples might be:

    Has this ever happened to me?

    How would I feel in this situation?

    Why does the person feel this way?

    What would I do?

    How do I feel about this person?

A Read the following paragraph. As you read, stop and think about the questions in parentheses. This will help you to connect your experiences with the reading.

It's a typical morning in San Diego, California. The sun is shining, so EP gets up and makes breakfast. Then he goes back to bed to listen to some music. (*Do you ever do this after breakfast?*) A few minutes later, he gets up again and has another breakfast. He has forgotten that he already ate. Some mornings he has three breakfasts. (*Is this normal?*) Fifteen years ago, EP suffered a serious illness. The illness destroyed part of his brain. As a result, he lost all memories from 1960 onwards. He cannot make new memories. (*Do you know any elderly people with memory problems?*) He doesn't remember he has a memory problem. He forgets he always forgets. His daughter lives nearby and looks after him. (*What would I do in this situation? Would I look after a family member with this type of problem?*) "He's happy all of the time. Very happy. I guess it's because he doesn't have any stress in his life," she says. (*Why doesn't he have any stress? Can someone with no memory really be happy?*)

B Share your answers to the questions in Exercise A with a partner.

C Work with a partner. Take turns reading *An Amazing Memory* out loud. At the end of each paragraph, stop and discuss the following questions.

1. Paragraph 1: How far can I remember into the past? What is my earliest memory?

2. Paragraph 2: How would I feel if I could remember the past like this?

3. Paragraph 3: Did I like school?

4. Paragraph 4: Am I better at remembering one type of information? Can I remember numbers better than names, for example?

5. Paragraph 5: Did I ever keep a diary? Do I like to read about the past?

6. Paragraph 6: Do I beat myself up about mistakes in the past?

VOCABULARY PRACTICE

Academic Vocabulary

A Find the words in bold in Reading 1. Use the context to help match each word with the correct definition.

_____ **1. unique** (Par. 3)	**a.** making you worry a lot
_____ **2. findings** (Par. 4)	**b.** very special and unusual
_____ **3. physically** (Par. 5)	**c.** decides after thinking about something
_____ **4. factors** (Par. 5)	**d.** results, conclusions
_____ **5. stressful** (Par. 6)	**e.** relating to the body
_____ **6. concludes** (Par. 6)	**f.** things that influence or lead to a situation

B The words in bold often appear with the words on the right. Find the words in bold in Reading 1. Circle the words that appear with them in the reading.

1. a **unique** _____ (Par. 3)   ability / opportunity

2. _____ **findings** (Par. 4)   different / interesting

3. **physically** _____ (Par. 5)   active / different

4. _____ **factors** (Par. 5)   important / two

5. _____ **stressful** (Par. 6)   more / less / very

6. _____ **concludes** (Par. 6)   she / the report / the expert

C Choose a word from the right column in Exercise B to complete each of the following sentences. More than one answer may be possible.

1. Taking the test was _____ **stressful** than she thought. She had prepared well and knew most of the answers, so she found it easy.

2. When Lee won a scholarship to a very good university overseas, he realized that this was a **unique** _____ to improve his English as well as gain a degree.

3. Young children like to be **physically** _____, so they need a lot of exercise and play outdoors.

4. _____ **concludes** that people use different parts of the brain to store, or keep, different types of memory.

5. Age, ability, and motivation are _____ **factors** in a person's memory skills.

6. Two different groups of experts looked at the same information and came up with _____ **findings**. One group found that as people get older, they can continue to improve their memory if they remain active. The other group found that older people cannot improve their memories.

Multiword Vocabulary

A Find the multiword vocabulary in bold in Reading 1. Use the context to help you complete each definition.

1. If you say something **is not the case** (Par. 2), you mean it is not _____.
   a. a good example
   b. true or correct

2. When you talk about **every single** (Par. 2) detail, you are emphasizing _____.
   a. one important detail in particular
   b. each one of several details

3. **On the other hand** (Par. 4) introduces _____.
   a. a contrast between two things or situations
   b. an additional similar point

4. If events or actions **shed light on** (Par. 5) something else, it means that they make it _____.
   a. brighter
   b. easier to understand

5. When I **give myself a break** (Par. 6), I _____.
   a. tell myself what I am doing wrong
   b. stop criticizing or saying negative things about myself

6. If I can't stop **beating myself up** (Par. 6), it means that I keep _____.
   a. thinking about my mistakes
   b. hitting myself

B Use the multiword vocabulary from the box to complete the following sentences.

beating myself up	gave him a break	shed light on
every single	on the other hand	was not the case

1. The research report can _____ why more girls are graduating from college in the United States than boys. It is very informative.

2. John thought the test was early that morning, but this _____. It was the following morning, so he had more time to prepare.

3. My friend told me that there was no point in _____ about the mistake I made in the final exam. I just had to try harder the next time.

4. Some people are very good at remembering people's names. _____, other people forget a new name as soon as they hear it.

5. After the accident, the police went over _____ piece of evidence in order to find out exactly what happened.

6. One of the students in the group forgot to do his part of a project. The others were not happy about this, but they _____ and helped him instead of criticizing him.

Use the Vocabulary

Write answers to the following questions. Use the words in bold in your answers. Then share your answers with a partner.

1. What kind of things do you find **stressful** at school? How do you relax in these situations?

2. What kinds of jobs require a person to be **physically** strong? Could you do any of these jobs?

3. When you make a mistake, are you the sort of person who **beats yourself up over it**, or do you simply forget it and move on?

4. Starting a new school or college can be difficult at first. Yet many students quickly get used to this new life and enjoy it. What **factors** make it easy for some students to quickly settle in and be happy at a new school?

5. Many students go to colleges and universities overseas. When they finish school, some of these students want to return to their home countries to begin their career. **On the other hand**, others would like to stay in the country where they studied and work there. What would you prefer to do if you had a choice?

6. We often hear the expression "Every individual is **unique**." Do you agree with this expression? In what ways are you unique?

7. Many teachers say that staying up late to study the night before a test is not helpful, but this **is not always the case**. Some students think it is a good idea to do this. What do you think?

THINK AND DISCUSS

Work in a small group. Use the information in the reading and your own ideas to discuss the following questions.

1. **Identify problems.** AJ describes her amazing memory as a burden. What does she mean by this? What examples does she give to support her statement?

2. **Evaluate.** Some people think that our memories are getting weaker because we use electronic devices to help us remember things. Do you think this is true? How has a smartphone, for example, affected your memory?

3. **Infer.** Why do you think the writer only uses the first two letters of AJ's name? Why not use her full name? What does this tell us about AJ?

Academic Vocabulary

to acquire	mental	a technique
a device	random	visual

Multiword Vocabulary

to back up something	in the space of
the first to admit	let alone
to have a chance of	to take a deep breath

Reading Preview

A **Preview.** Read the title. Look at the photos and read the captions. Then discuss the following questions with a partner or in a small group.

1. An athlete is a person who trains for a sport. What do we mean by the term *mental athlete*?

2. What kind of "sports" does a mental athlete train for?

3. Do you think you would make a good mental athlete? Explain your answer.

B **Topic vocabulary.** The following words appear in Reading 2. Look at the words and answer the questions with a partner.

athletes	contestant	national
audience	judge	recite
champion	memorize	training

1. Which words are about improving your memory?

2. Which words describe jobs or roles that people have?

3. Which words are adjectives? What do they mean?

C **Predict.** What do you think this reading will be about? Discuss each word in Exercise B and predict how it may relate to the reading.

Chester Santos, a U.S. Memory Championship winner, stands in front of signs showing Wimbledon tennis champions. He uses the signs to teach memorization skills.

We all want to improve our memory. What is the best way to do this? Meet someone who has found a way to train his memory to remember extraordinary things.

Joshua Foer

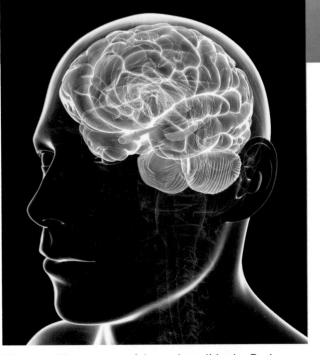

Figure 1. Hippocampus (shown in red) in the Brain

H e put in his earplugs[1] and the competition hall went quiet. In front of him were 99 photos next to names. For 15 minutes he memorized as many of the names as possible. Then the judge took the names away. He wrote down as many as he could—a total of 107 first and last names. He moved on to the next event. Here he had 15 minutes to learn and recite 400 random words. He took a deep breath. Once again, he made it and advanced to the final round. He had five minutes to memorize two

----

[1] *earplugs:* small things you put in your ears to keep out noise

decks of cards. As he said each card in the correct order, the audience was silent. Then Joshua Foer heard, "We have a new United States Memory Champion!" He had won.

Joshua Foer would be the first to admit that for some things he has an average memory. He regularly forgets where he has put his car keys. He forgets phone numbers of close friends. Yet in the space of a year, he trained his memory and won a national competition. How did he do it?

Foer, a journalist, first entered the world of mental athletes in 2005. He was writing a story about the U.S. Memory Championship. Once there, he watched one contestant in amazement. Ed Cooke memorized 252 random digits[2] as easily as one simple telephone number. Afterwards, Cooke explained that his memory was actually quite average. He just knew *how* to remember. Cooke offered to teach Foer, and the adventure began.

It turns out that mental athletes use techniques from 2,500 years ago in ancient Greece. These techniques, called mnemonic devices, can help anyone improve their memory. Most of these devices require a person to connect a mental picture to the information he or she must remember. For example, a friend introduces a new person. As you repeat this person's name, you create a mental picture. You think of where you are and what color shirt you are wearing. If you attach this visual image to the new name, you are more likely to remember it later on.

Science backs up the effectiveness of mnemonic devices. Research shows that you can develop your brain with memory exercises just as athletes develop muscles with physical exercises. The hippocampus is a part of the brain that affects memory. (See Figure 1.) Dr. Majid Fotuhi explains, "When you've acquired the skills, you're more likely to use your memory more often. And the more you use your memory, the stronger your hippocampus gets." With practice, these mnemonic devices can turn an average memory into a very powerful tool.

At first, Foer didn't think he had a chance of getting to the finals[3]—let alone winning.

---

[2] *digits:* any series of numbers made up of numerals 0–9

[3] *finals:* the last and most important part of a competition

He decided to compete anyway. And he won the championship because he learned how to memorize. Has this training changed his life? Maybe. When he uses memory techniques, he does remember things more easily. But he is still a man of average memory. A few days after he became the U.S Memory Champion, he went out to dinner with some friends. Afterwards, he said goodnight and took the subway home. As he walked into his house, he suddenly realized he had driven to the restaurant. Foer had forgotten his car.

Andy Pope

THE MEMORY COP

One dark evening in England, a police officer was walking on a quiet street. A young man passed him. "I know that face," thought the officer. He stopped the man and questioned him. He was right. The police were looking for this person. He was wanted for robbery. How did the officer know the man's face? He had seen it in a black-and-white photo one year earlier.

The police officer is Andy Pope. He has an amazing memory for faces. Every morning, he looks at photos of suspects. Then he goes out and walks around his community. He looks at hundreds of people's faces during the day and some of them match the photos of the suspects. So far, he has identified 250 criminals. According to his wife, Andy may have an incredible memory for faces, but she says he is not very good at remembering anything else.

READING COMPREHENSION

Big Picture

A Read the following pairs of sentences. In each pair, write *MI* next to the main idea and *SD* next to the supporting detail.

Paragraph 1

_____ **a.** Foer won the U.S. memory competition.

_____ **b.** In the competition, Foer had to remember hundreds of names and numbers.

Paragraph 2

_____ **a.** It took Foer one year to prepare for the competition.

_____ **b.** Despite having an average memory, Foer became a memory champion.

Paragraph 3

_____ **a.** Foer met Ed Cooke while he was working on a story.

_____ **b.** Writing a story about memory led Foer to enter the competition.

Paragraph 4

_____ **a.** A mnemonic device is a technique that helps you improve memory.

_____ **b.** Attaching a visual image to a name is an example of a mnemonic device.

Paragraph 5

_____ **a.** The hippocampus is the part of the brain that affects memory.

_____ **b.** Scientific findings show that practice improves memory.

Paragraph 6

_____ **a.** Foer still uses memory techniques.

_____ **b.** Foer won the championship because he learned how to improve his memory.

B Compare answers to Exercise A with a partner. Then write a sentence expressing the main idea of the whole reading.

Close-Up

A Choose the best answer for each of the following questions.

1. Reread the first sentence of paragraph 1. Why do you think the writer begins with this sentence?
   a. It explains that the hall is very quiet.
   b. It introduces the importance of earplugs.
   c. It is exciting and encourages the reader to continue.
   d. It is the first thing that happens in a series of events.

2. Which of the following actions shows that Foer was probably nervous during the completion?
   a. He put in his earplugs.
   b. He took a deep breath.
   c. He recited each card.
   d. He advanced to the final round.

3. Which statement is *not* correct, according to paragraph 2?
   a. Foer knows that his memory is average.
   b. He often forgets little things such as phone numbers and car keys.
   c. Before his training, he believed his memory was better than most people's.
   d. For 12 months, Foer worked hard to improve his memory.

4. Why was Foer amazed by Ed Cooke, according to paragraph 3?
   a. Cooke explained that he had just an average memory.
   b. Cooke offered to help Foer train for a national competition.
   c. Cooke quickly learned and recited over two hundred numbers.
   d. Cooke was a contestant in a national competition.

5. Which is the best definition of a *mnemonic device*?
   a. a technique that began 2,500 years ago in ancient Greece
   b. a specific technique that helps people improve their memory
   c. connecting a mental picture to important information
   d. attaching a visual image to a new name

6. What logical conclusion can you make from paragraph 5?
   a. The brain is like a muscle because it can be trained.
   b. Everyone can become a national memory champion.
   c. Practice is not important for improving memory.
   d. It is very difficult to improve your memory.

7. According to the short extra reading, "The Memory Cop," on page 181, what is similar about Foer and Pope?
   a. They both use mnemonic devices to improve their memory.
   b. They can remember some things very well, but forget other things.
   c. Neither man has to work hard to improve his memory.
   d. Both men have autobiographical memories.

B Compare answers to Exercise A with a partner. If you have different answers, reread the text to find the correct one.

Reading Skill

Identifying Contrast

A contrast refers to two different ideas. Writers often use a contrast to introduce unexpected or surprising information.

Example:

Although Foer only had average memory, after just one year of training he became the U.S. Memory Champion.

In this sentence, the two contrasting ideas are the following:

Foer had an average memory. He won the U.S. Memory competition.

The writer uses the signal word *although* to introduce this contrast.

Writers use these signal words and phrases to introduce contrasts:

| but | yet | however | even though | on the other hand | in contrast |
| whereas | different | differences | | | |

A Read the following paragraph. Underline signal words that introduce contrasts. Then answer the questions below.

Scientists are interested in the differences between short-term and long-term memory. Short-term memory refers to your ability to remember something for a few minutes, whereas long-term memory refers to remembering something for a much longer time. Remembering a phone number while you look for a pen to write it down is an example of short-term memory. In contrast, remembering how to look up something on the Internet is an example of long-term memory. There are significant differences between these two types of memory. Short-term memory only lasts from a few minutes to a few days. However, long-term memory can last a lifetime if the person regularly thinks about the information. Another difference is space. The brain has less space for short-term memory. In fact, the average person can only recall between five and nine items in the short-term. On the other hand, there is no limit to how much you can remember long-term.

1. The writer is contrasting two things in the opening sentence. What are they?

_____

_____

2. What signal word first introduces this contrast?

_____

_____

3. Find the phrase *in contrast*. What two differences does it introduce?

_____

_____

4. Find two more contrasts. Write them below.

_____

_____

B Scan both Reading 1 and 2 to find the following contrast signal words. Then read the sentences around the signal words to find the two contrasting ideas. Use this information to complete the following chart. More than one answer is possible in some cases.

Signal Word/ Phrase	Idea 1	Idea 2
but		
however		
in contrast		
on the other hand		
yet		

VOCABULARY PRACTICE

Academic Vocabulary

A Find the words in the box in Reading 2. Use the context and the words in parentheses to help you choose the correct word to complete the following sentences.

mental (Par. 3)	techniques (Par. 4)	visual (Par. 4)
random (Par. 3)	devices (Par. 4)	acquired (Par. 5)

1. When I meet a new person, I try to think of a clear _____ (relating to sight) picture of that person. This image helps me remember the person's name.

2. The teacher used very effective _____ (ways of doing something) for teaching pronunciation. For example, students used a computer program to practice speaking clearly on the phone.

3. When I was in college, I _____ (learned, developed) new skills such as how to research and remember important information.

4. A(n) _____ (relating to the mind) health counselor talks with individuals about how to deal with stress and face challenges in their lives.

5. We can connect to the Internet with many _____ (things developed for a particular purpose) such as laptops and mobile phones.

6. The teacher selected a(n) _____ (chosen without a plan) group of students and asked them to prepare a presentation for the following week.

B Read the following sentences and choose the best word to complete each one. The correct word often appears with the word in bold. Write the word on the line.

1. _____ **devices** such as phones and laptops allow people to work not only from home, but while they are traveling.
   a. Cheap   b. Mobile   c. Tiny

2. Writing down information is a _____ **technique** to help you remember it.
   a. new   b. scientific   c. useful

3. The doctor was very concerned about the patient's **mental** _____.
   a. health   b. brain   c. advantages

4. The new movie has amazing **visual** _____. It is about life on Mars, and it looks very real.
   a. parts   b. actors   c. images

5. The researchers chose a **random** _____ of people and asked them to participate in an experiment.
   a. family   b. group   c. choice

6. The police **acquired** new _____ about the accident. When they studied the driver's phone, they found she was talking on the phone while driving.
   a. information   b. funds   c. names

Multiword Vocabulary

(A) Find the multiword vocabulary in bold in Reading 2. Use the context to help you complete each definition.

1. He **took a deep breath** (Par. 1) means he _____.
   - **a.** tried to calm down by breathing in
   - **b.** breathed normally

2. If you are **the first to admit** (Par. 2) something, you are _____.
   - **a.** the first person to enter an event such as a movie
   - **b.** willing to say something is true

3. **In the space of** (Par. 2) refers to _____.
   - **a.** a small place
   - **b.** a period of time

4. When new research **backs up** (Par. 5) a previous finding, it means _____.
   - **a.** the research provides more evidence to show it is true
   - **b.** the information is not accurate

5. If you didn't think you **had a chance of** (Par. 6) doing something, you didn't _____.
   - **a.** know how to do something
   - **b.** think you would be able to do it

6. When we use **let alone** (Par. 6) in a sentence, it means _____.
   - **a.** definitely not
   - **b.** to leave someone by himself

(B) Compare answers to Exercise A with a partner. Then choose the correct multiword vocabulary from the box to complete the following sentences.

back up	in the space of	take a deep breath
have a chance of	let alone	the first to admit

1. Atsuko didn't think she would even pass the test, _____ score over 90 percent!

2. The university was able to _____ the findings with results from several research projects.

3. Before the concert, the piano teacher told her student to remember to _____ and calm down before she started to play the piece.

4. The two friends have very good grades and test scores from high school, so they both _____ getting into a good university.

5. The storm was so strong that _____ an hour, many homes and businesses were completely destroyed.

6. My friend is not always _____ that he has made a mistake, but he always says he is sorry in the end.

Use the Vocabulary

Write answers to the following questions. Use the words in bold in your sentences.
Then share your answers with a partner.

1. What **useful techniques** do you have to prepare for final exams? How do you calm yourself down once the exam begins? For example, do you **take a deep breath**? Count to 10?

2. These days, most people own multiple **mobile devices**. What devices do you own? What do you use these devices for?

3. Think about a class you are taking right now. Do you **have a good chance of** passing this class? Why or why not?

4. One mnemonic device is to make a **mental** picture of someone when you meet him or her for the first time. Do you do this? Does it help you remember names? What other methods do you use to remember information?

5. Are you **the first to admit** when you make a mistake? Or are you hesitant to admit an error?

6. Writers use supporting details to **back up** their main ideas. Do you sometimes find it difficult to think of these details when writing a paper? Where do you get your information from?

THINK AND DISCUSS

Work in a small group. Use the information in the reading and your own ideas to discuss the following questions.

1. **Summarize.** Describe how Joshua Foer became the U.S. memory champion.

2. **Evaluate.** Both Cooke and Foer claim that they have average memories. They just learned how to improve their memories. Do you agree with them that anyone can do this?

3. **Apply knowledge.** How do you remember information for important tests? Do you stay up late the night before? Make lots of notes? Repeat the facts out loud?

Vocabulary Review

A Complete the paragraphs with the vocabulary below that you have studied in the unit.

backs up	unique opportunity
the first to admit	useful techniques
in the space of	visual image
mobile devices	was not the case

National Geographic offered journalist and memory champion Joshua Foer a _____ . They wanted him
1
to go to the Congo, in Africa, to write about a group of people. The challenge? Foer needed to learn Lingua, the language spoken by this group. Foer turned to the Internet for help. He thought there would be many online resources. This, however, _____ . In fact, all he found was an old English–Lingua dictionary.
2
This was a problem because Foer is _____ that learning a language is not
3
easy for him. So, who did he turn to for help? His old memory teacher, Ed Cooke.

Cooke was designing apps (software applications) for _____ such as cell
4
phones. His apps made memorizing information fun and not stressful. The apps taught many _____ to help people improve their memory. Foer used the apps to learn the
5
vocabulary from the Lingua dictionary. He made a _____ for each word. He
6
also studied for short periods of time. Science _____ this approach. The brain
7
remembers more if you study information for a short time and then practice recalling that information. _____ two and a half months, Foer memorized the entire Lingua
8
dictionary. Did this help him communicate? One day in the Congo, he didn't understand an old man. Foer asked a translator to help him. "Te, te, oyoka malamu," the old man said. "No, no, you understand well." And that made Foer feel good.

B Compare answers to Exercise A with a partner. Then discuss the following questions.

How do you think the apps helped Foer learn the vocabulary? Do you use mobile devices to help you understand words that you don't understand?

C Complete the following sentences in a way that shows that you understand the meaning of the words in bold.

1. Being a teenager can be **stressful** because teenagers worry about _____ .

2. The athlete **took a deep breath** and _____ .

3. The accident report **shed light on** _____ .

4. Why do some children learn to read more easily than others? There are many reasons but one **important factor** is _____ .

D Work with a partner and write four sentences that include any four of the vocabulary items below. You may use any verb tense and make nouns plural if you want.

acquire information	experts conclude	physically active
have a chance of	mental health	random groups

Connect the Readings

A Readings 1 and 2 are about two unusual people. The readings discuss how AJ and Joshua Foer both have an unusual ability to remember things. Yet these two individuals are very different. Read the following questions. Check (✓) the box to indicate the correct answers.

	AJ	Joshua Foer
Who claims to have an average memory?		
Who first realized that he or she had an extraordinary memory as a child?		
Whose memory affects him or her every single day?		
Who scores well on memory tests?		
Who has an autobiographical memory?		
Who can control his or her memory?		
Who uses very old mnemonic devices to help him or her remember?		
Who participates in memory competitions?		

B Choose four differences from the chart above. Write sentences describing these differences. Use signal words and phrases from the Reading Skill on page 183.

1. *Although* _____

2. _____

3. _____

4. _____

C Discuss the following questions with a partner. Use your understanding of the readings and your own ideas.

1. Imagine you are helping a friend prepare for an important test. Make a list of things your friend can do to learn and remember the information.

2. Look at the vocabulary lists on pages 170 and 178. Choose five words from the academic or the multiword vocabulary that are still difficult for you. Think of a visual image for each item. What visual images have you chosen? Do they help you remember?

3. Do you think electronic devices in the future will change the way students learn a language?

VOCABULARY INDEX

The following words and phrases are studied in *Reading and Vocabulary Focus 1*. Each vocabulary item is listed according to which unit and reading it appears in. For example, a word or phrase listed as **U1 R1** appears in the first reading of unit 1. If a word is in the Academic Word List, it is listed as **AWL**.

CREDITS

Text Sources

The following sources were consulted when writing the readings for *Reading and Vocabulary Focus 1*.

6–7: "Bus2Antartica," http://travel.nationalgeographic.com/travel/bus2antarctica/; additional source: National Geographic Live!, "Andrew Evans: Digital Nomad," www.youtube.com/watch2v=04mgXCI2LO; **14–15:** "The Best Job in the World," http://natgeotv.com/asia/the-best-job-in-the-world; additional source: "Best Job Winner Takes up Role," http://news.bbc.co.uk/2/hi/uk_news/england/hampshire/8127914.stm; **20:** "Adventurers of the Year Explorer: Ed Stafford," Ryan Bradley, Ed Stafford: http://adventure.nationalgeographic.com/adventure/adventurers-of-the-year/ed-stafford-2010/; additional source: http://www.nationalgeographic.com/radio/episodes/NGW-1102/ngwkd1102-hour2_seg2.mp3; **26–28:** "Fire Season" by Neil Shea, July 2008: http://ngm.nationalgeographic.com/2008/07/fire-season/shea-text; additional source: http://abcnews.go.com/Technology/story?id=119700; **36:** "Bangladesh: The Coming Storm" by Don Belt, May 2011: http://ngm.nationalgeographic.com/2011/05/bangladesh/belt-text; **48–49:** "Saving Lives with Solar-powered Lights," http://www.cnn.com/2010/LIVING/02/11/cnnheroes.wadongo/; **56–57:** "Big Ideas; Little Packages" by Margaret G. Zackowitz, November 2010: http://ngm.nationalgeographic.com/big-idea/16/little-packages; additional sources: http://natgeotv.com/me/planet-mechanics/galleries/electric-water-taxi; "Solar Plane Completes First Intercontinental Flight" by Brian Handwerk, May 2012, National Geographic News: http://news.nationalgeographic.com/news/energy/2012/05/pictures/120531-solar-plane-intercontinental-flight/; **68–69:** "Eat less meat to avoid climate disaster, Study Warns" by Suzanne Goldenberg: http://www.theguardian.com/environment/2012/apr/13/less-meat-prevent-climate-change; additional sources: "Food Shortages could force world into vegetarianism, warn scientists" by John Vidal, The Guardian, August 26, 2012; "The Global Food Crisis" by Joel K. Bourne Jr., National Geographic Magazine, June 2009: http://ngm.nationalgeographic.com/2009/06/cheap-food/bourne-text; http://www.nytimes.com/2013/08/06/science/a-lab-grown-burger-gets-a-taste-test.html; **78–79:** "Urban Farming is Growing a Green Future" by Graham Gotham: http://environment.nationalgeographic.com/environment/photos/urban-farming/#/earth-day-urban-farming-truck-farm_51634_600x450.jpg; additional source: "Truck Farm," a DVD by Wicked Delight; **84:** "Learning from urban farmer and compost king Will Allen" by David Braun, October 2010: http://newswatch.nationalgeographic.com/2010.10/21/will-allen-urban-farming/; **90–91:** "Artic Redwood Fossils are Clues to Ancient Climates" by Bijal P. Trivedi, March 2002: http://news.nationalgeographic.com/news/2002/03/0326_020326_TVredwoods.html; additional source: "Drying of the West" by Robert Kunzig, February 2002: http://ngm.nationalgeographic.com/2008/02/drying-west/kunzig-text; **104:** "Trees Rings Suggest Roman World was Drier than Thought" by Fred Pearce: http://www.newscientist.com/article/dn22040-tree-rings-suggest-roman-world-was-warmer-than-thought.html; **110–111:** "From Garbage to Gold" by Stacy Perman: http://www.businessweek.com/stories/2006-08-16/from-garbage-to-gold; "Living in a Box," http://environment.nationalgeographic.com/environment/sustainable-earth/pictures-amsterdam-shipping-container-homes/; "Keetwonen," http://www.tempohousing.com/projects/keetwonen.html; **124:** "The Rock Garden" http://www.pbs.org/independentlens/offthemap/html/travelogue_artist_3.htm?true; **130–131:** "Orphans No More" by Charles Siebert, September 2011: http://ngm.nationalgeographic.com/2011/09/orphan-

elephants/siebert-text/2; additional source: http://ngm.nationalgeographic.com/2011/09/
orphan-elephants/orphan-elephant-video; **138–139:** "Racing to Protect the Koalas" by
Mark Jenkins: National Geographic Magazine, May 2012: http://ngm.nationalgeographic.
com/2012/05/koala-rescue/jenkins-text; **144:** "Krithi Karanth, Conservation Biologist,"
http://www.nationalgeographic.com/explorers/bios/krithi-karanth/; **150–151:** "New Island
Born" by Richard A. Lovett, January 2012: http://news.nationalgeographic.com/news/
travelnews/2012/01/120119-new-island-yemen-earth-nasa-science-space/; **158–159:** "Floating
Golf Courses, Villas And Hotels All Part Of Sinking Maldives Plan To Hover Above Rising Sea
Level" by Mark Johanson: http://www.ibtimes.com/floating-golf-courses-villas-and-hotels-all-
part-sinking-maldives-plan-hover-above-rising-sea-levels; additional sources: "As the World
Sinks" by Costas Christ: http://travel.nationalgeographic.com/travel/traveler-magazine/tales-
from-the-frontier/maldives/; **172–173:** "Remember This" by Joshua Foer, National Geographic
Magazine, November 2007: http://ngm.nationalgeographic.com/print/2007/11/memory/foer-
text; **180–181:** "Moonwalking with Einstein" by J. Foer, Penguin Press, 2011; additional source:
http://www.telegraph.co.uk/news/uknews/crime/9499457/Memory-Cop-Andy-Pope-fighting-
crime-with-his-memory-for-faces.html; **188:** "How I Learned a Language in 22 Hours" by Joshua
Foer: http://www.theguardian.com/education/2012/nov/09/learn-language-in-three-months

Art Credits

Cover: Hiroyuki Matsumoto/Photographer's Choice/Getty Images; **iii:** (t) MIKE THEISS/National Geographic Creative; **iii:** (c) Ekkachai Pholrojpanya/Flickr/Getty Images; **iii:** (b) Michael Melford/National Geographic Creative; **iv:** (t) SHIVJI JOSHI/National Geographic Creative; **iv:** (c) Mario Tama/Getty Images; **iv:** (b) OLIVIER MAIRE/EPA/Newscom; **v:** (t) JOEL SARTORE/National Geographic Creative; **v:** (c) STEVE AND DONNA O'MEARA/National Geographic Creative; **v:** (b) DAI SHULIN/EPA/Newscom; **vi:** (t) Michael Melford/National Geographic Creative; **vi:** (b) MARTIN BERNETTI/AFP/Getty Images/Newscom; **vii:** (l) National Geographic Channel; **vii:** (c) AP Images/PR NEWSWIRE; **vii:** (r) Charles Ellena/Bloomberg via Getty Images; **viii:** David Leahy/Iconica/Getty Images; **ix:** P J Hendrikse/MCT/ Newscom; **2–3:** MIKE THEISS/National Geographic Creative; **4–5:** PAUL NICKLEN/National Geographic Creative; **6–7, 11:** ANDREW EVANS/National Geographic Creative; **12–13:** PAUL CHESLEY/National Geographic Creative; **14:** TORSTEN BLACKWOOD/AFP/Getty Images; **15:** SP-PIC/Fotolia LLC; **18:** JULIA SUMERLING/National Geographic Creative; **20:** PETE MCBRIDE/National Geographic Creative; **22–23:** Ekkachai Pholrojpanya/Flickr/Getty Images; **24–25:** Mike Stone/REUTERS; **26–27:** MARK THIESSEN/National Geographic Creative; **27:** (tr) Maria Ismawi/Flickr/Getty images; **28:** U.S. Air Force/digital version by Science Faction/Science Faction/Getty images; **33:** Rick Wilking/REUTERS; **34–35:** Andrew Biraj/REUTERS; **36–37:** JAMES P. BLAIR/National Geographic Creative; **37:** (cr) MCNULTY, WILLIAM E./National Geographic Creative; **42:** Daniel Munoz/REUTERS; **44–45:** Michael Melford/National Geographic Creative; **46–47:** LYNN JOHNSON/National Geographic Creative; **48:** (b) Tiffany Rose/WireImage/Getty Images; **48–49:** TONY KARUMBA/AFP/ Getty Images; **54–55:** MARTIN BERNETTI/AFP/Getty Images/Newscom; **56:** (cr) AP Images/ PR NEWSWIRE; **56:** (bl) Olaf Speier/Shutterstock.com; **56–57:** Charles Ellena/Bloomberg via Getty Images; **61:** David Leahy/Iconica/Getty Images; **62–63:** P J Hendrikse/MCT/ Newscom; **64–65:** SHIVJI JOSHI/National Geographic Creative; **66–67:** CHRIS JOHNS/ National Geographic Creative; **68:** Tom Merton/OJO Images/Getty Images; **69:** (bl) POOL New/Reuters; **72:** (br) Donald Erickson/E+/Getty Images; **75:** CB2/ZOB/WENN.com/ Newscom; **76–77:** DIANE COOK AND LEN JENSHEL/National Geographic Creative; **78–79:** Linda Rosier/NY Daily News Archive/Getty Image; **84:** Benny Sieu/MCT/Newscom; **86–87:** Mario Tama/Getty Images; **88–89:** IRA BLOCK/National Geographic Creative; **90–91:** RENAULT Philippe/hemis.fr/Alamy; **96–97:** MICHAEL NICHOLS/National Geographic Creative; **98:** ROBERT SISSON/National Geographic Creative; **101:** BRUCE DALE/National Geographic Creative; **104:** malcolm park/Britain On View/Getty Images; **106–107:** OLIVIER MAIRE/EPA/ Newscom; **108–109:** AP Images/Ed Wray; **110, 111:** Mike Siegel/KRT/Newscom; **116–117:** Simon Balson/Alamy; **118:** (t) Paul O'Driscoll/Bloomberg via Getty Images; **118:** (br) PETE RYAN/ National Geographic Creative; **123:** Horizons WWP/Alamy; **124:** MANAN VATSYAYANA/AFP/ Getty Images; **126–127:** JOEL SARTORE/National Geographic Creative; **128–129, 130:** MICHAEL NICHOLS/National Geographic Creative; **136–137, 138:** JOEL SARTORE/National Geographic Creative; **142:** Michael Sewell/Photolibrary/Getty Images; **144:** (t) MICHAEL NICHOLS/National Geographic Creative; **144:** (tr) Shekar Dattatri; **146–147:** STEVE AND DONNA O'MEARA/National Geographic Creative; **148–149:** NASA; **150–151, 152:** PATRICK MCFEELEY/National Geographic Creative; **156–157:** Mohamed Abdulla Shafeeg/Flickr Open/Getty Images; **158:** (bl) Gabriel Sperandio/Flickr/Getty Images; **158–159:** Ho New/Reuters; **159:** (bl) Fuse/Getty Images; **162:** Chris

Hepburn/Photodisc/Getty Images; **165:** MARWAN NAAMANI/AFP/Getty Images; **168–169:** DAI SHULIN/EPA/Newscom; **170–171:** WILLIAM ALBERT ALLARD/National Geographic Creative; **172:** Nicole Kucera/Flickr Select/Getty Images; **178–179:** AP Images/Jeff Chiu; **180:** (t) Manuel Silvestri/Polaris/Newscom; **180:** (br) SCIEPRO/Science Photo Library/Getty Images; **181:** NEWSTEAM; **187:** THOMAS SAMSON/AFP/Getty Images; **188:** Christopher Lane/Contour/Getty Images